ESOTERIC MIND POWER

by

VERNON HOWARD

NEW LIFE FOUNDATION
Pine, Arizona 85544

Fourth Printing 1994
Copyright 1973 by Vernon Howard

ISBN 0-911203-27-3
Library of Congress Catalog Card Number 73-83914

FOR INFORMATION ON CLASSES, BOOKS,
TAPES AND VIDEO CASSETTES, WRITE:
NEW LIFE
PO BOX 2230
PINE, ARIZONA 85544

CONTENTS

HOW TO USE THIS BOOK FOR RICH REWARDS

This book contains everything you need to know for winning a totally new and inspiring life. Here you will find a grand summary of all the powerful truths discovered by the great minds of ancient times and of today. Eastern teachings and Western wisdoms are blended into one volume, easy to understand and just as easy to apply personally.

Study these ideas with a relaxed mind, yet with enthusiastic interest. Use them just as if this were the first time you have tried to change your life for the better. Do this while remembering the practical power of these classic wisdoms. What would be the perfect definition of the phrase *practical action*? Certainly it is *to act in a way which is truly and lastingly best for you.* You will soon be adventuring with this kind of practical action. You will be shown just what to do and how to do it.

Many of these ideas may astonish you. Wonderful! Astonishment opens the door which permits self-newness to enter with all its riches. What if you truly understood how life really works? What if you were forever free of both inner and outer conflict? Would it not cause astonishment to glimpse these lofty ways? They exist. They appear to anyone who desires them deeply and persistently.

Use these action-programs: 1. As you read, select those sentences and ideas which impress you in particular. Write them down, each on its separate slip of paper, and concentrate on the single message for a few days. This sets

9

an idea under your mental magnifying glass, which brings out its full excellence. 2. Put these dynamic principles into daily practice in the home or office or anywhere else. Let them enter into all of your human relations. Remember, the purpose of these esoteric principles is to make you a new person who casually turns every day into a refreshing day. Invite them to succeed in this and they will surely do so.

You can proceed alone, or with others, or with a combination of both methods. Each has its unique advantages. Solitary work is excellent for strengthening valuable self-reliance. Group meetings, such as the *Vernon Howard Study Groups*, provide an exchange of helpful information. The experiences of various study-groups mentioned in this book will benefit you.

Your reading will introduce you to dozens of men and women who have come with their personal problems and questions. You may have asked the same questions, if so, the answers which banished their difficulties can also aid you.

What do we mean by the word *esoteric?* Nothing mysterious. It refers to those higher truths and to those authentic powers which change and uplift everyone who receives them.

Delightful feelings will arise as these truths are absorbed over the coming weeks. It is like a bird which soars freely by drifting into oneness with uplifting breezes. So let yourself go, remembering that Truth by its very nature is both kindly and powerful, having only one aim—your inner success and happiness.

Vernon Howard

Chapter 1

HEALING AND REFRESHMENT
CAN NOW BE YOURS

Why do you put up with it? You know what I mean.
Why on earth do you go along with what is bothering you?
Would you put up with a treacherous and harmful acquaintance? Of course not. Whatever it is, you don't have to put
up with it; not any more. You can take action. I am not
referring to action against outer conditions, for that changes
nothing. I am speaking of inner action, which changes
everything. Don't put up with it any longer. Act now.

In a class for self-enlightenment, everyone was asked
to supply a declaration of independence from society's folly. Each student was to speak as if to society itself. Richard W., a city employee, contributed the following: "If you
want to go through life scared and hostile, that is your privilege—but leave me out. I have found an entirely new way
to live."

Suppose you are walking past an athletic stadium when
some players race out and tug you back into their game. You
try to explain your unfamiliarity with the rules, but they
only scream for you to play, to run with the ball, to score
points. This is man's position on earth. He feels compelled
to play the game, but has no idea of what he is supposed
to do. No wonder he feels lost! The aim of this book is to
show you how to score worthwhile points for yourself.

What is the magnificent message all the great teachers
have given the world? It is the good news of self-freedom.
Man is chained by illusions, but can lose his chains. Even

11

though he cannot even ask the right questions, mental receptivity can enable him to hear the right answers. This
good news is for all who are worried and weary. The
teachers declare, "There *is* another way. Come, let me
show it to you."

One day, Count Leo Tolstoy was walking away from his
home to perform an errand, when a sudden understanding
came to him: the errand was unnecessary. With this
pleasant realization, he turned around and went back
home. When spiritual insight reveals that frantic searchings for happiness, that self-concern, that false guilt, are
all unnecessary, we are instantly relieved of all useless
and tiring errands in life.

Humanity's great tragedy is its inability to realize what
is truly practical. Only esoteric mind-power can produce
anything practical. Look at the impractical way people meet
each other. Watch their nervousness and uncertainty. So remind yourself constantly of the connection between these
principles and right living. It is strange how a man complains,
"Everything went wrong today," without seeing the link
between his mind and what happened to him. So nothing is
more practical than to see the connection between our minds
and our experiences.

YOU CAN KNOW THE ANSWERS TO LIFE

A new insight, even a small one, arouses tremendous
energy for self-elevation. James L. saw that we really do
attract people and experiences which occupy the same
psychic level as our own. Also noticing how he constantly attracted negative events, James served his own interests by raising his level, which attracted higher and happier
conditions. His very insight provided strength for the task.

The answers to life are known. Jesus and Buddha knew.
In their own ways, so did Emerson and Tolstoy, Spinoza

and Schopenhauer, Lao-tse and Marcus Aurelius. These men were first and last practical men, the truly practical men, for only trueness is practical. What they knew, you can also know. No one is denied, everyone is welcomed. Your part is to become aware of your welcome.

Meister Eckhart, the German mystic, provided this excellent guide: ''Be willing to be a beginner every single morning.'' Do this and you will not lose anything already gained, to the contrary, you will gain much more. Eleanor H. saw how this attitude made her more receptive to her own good, which led to a new sense of freedom from daily pressure.

You don't have to complicate your thinking toward these ideas. Simple words will do. You are working on yourself because happiness is better than misery. You are abandoning your old ways because it will keep you out of trouble. You are welcoming new principles because it is the sensible thing to do. Simplicity itself is your guiding star.

No action is more fascinating than the action of self-transformation. Nothing on earth can compare with its drama or its value. In Athens, one day, Diogenes was asked whether he was going to attend the athletic contests at the local arena. Diogenes replied that his favorite contest was to wrestle with and to win over his own nature.

A man's life begins to change when he honestly doubts his life as it is—doubts his values, ambitions, activities, his knowledge. It takes courage to reach this stage, for the man realizes that the old building must be destroyed to make way for the new structure. When a man gets tired of pretending that everything is all right, honest doubt begins its good work of truly making everything all right.

Many people feel they lack the intelligence to find the higher way, but this is merely a misunderstanding. Intelligence has nothing to do with college degrees or public fame or even the reading of many books. Authentic intelligence is the willingness to exchange fancy for fact, to exchange imaginary self-pictures for healthy self-insight. Think of true intelligence as being an individual wish for rightness, after which you need never give it another thought.

ACCEPT THIS INVITATION TO HEALING

Whenever meeting an idea you do not understand, simply ask yourself, "What does this mean?" Then, reflect upon it easily, quietly, making sure you are not led toward an answer you unconsciously *wanted* to find. Hold all questions in a suspended position in your mind in this way, and eventually they will drop down into your understanding.

Carl A. gained ground by becoming conscious of a certain mechanical reaction from his mind. He saw how he often rejected anything he could not understand or which was unfamiliar to his thinking habits. Awareness of this opened his mind to a wealth of new ideas, for example, he saw how rightness and easiness go together.

A prosperous Englishman was kidnapped and held for ransom in another part of his own city. To induce feelings of despair, his kidnappers created several illusions to make him think he was in a distant Dutch town. He was served Dutch food and the Dutch language was spoken outside his door. But his kidnappers were careless just long enough for him to catch a glimpse outside, which revealed his true location. Stengthened by this knowledge, he managed to escape. Likewise, we are separated from our true good only by illusions. We escape by seeing through them, which is why *seeing* is our great aim.

The advice of man-made systems to psychic prisoners can be summarized, "Find some pretty toys to keep your mind off your prison cell." Esotericism says: "Have the courage to abandon your fragile toys and channel your natural intelligence toward escape from the cell. Start believing in yourself even when you can see no reason for it, even though you have committed a thousand blunders, even while criticized for your attempts to do so."

The usual kind of public discussions about human betterment can lead nowhere, but few see it, for few see through the human masquerade. Everyone taking part in such discussions will speak from an imaginary self which is frantically and futilely trying to prove its existence by sounding wise and compassionate. The only man worth listening to is the man who is not playing this unconscious trick on himself, and such a man is not found on every corner.

Somehow you sense, do you not, that the only man who can help you is the man who has found the way out for himself. But where do you find such a man? How will you recognize him as one who truly knows? Such a man represents the truth, and if you really want the truth, you will meet him, either in person or in his teachings.

An awakened man invites wandering mankind, "Come, let me show you a totally new way of life. Do not fear my message, for the truths you fear are the very truths which can save you from yourselves. Come with a quiet mind, come with the intention of receiving inner illumination. Come with a wish to be healed and you will be healed."

THE VALUE OF GROUP MEETINGS

What do the great teachers mean by saying man is asleep? It is very simple. To be asleep means to suffer, to be burdened by hidden fears and conflicts, to not live from one's own pure nature, but to slavishly imitate foolish public customs. To be awake means to have a free and spontaneous spirit, to be one with universal laws and therefore opposed by nothing, to see life as it truly is, and to know that all is well.

Suppose a patient consults a doctor about an illness, to hear the doctor say, "Very well. I will prescribe some medicine for your neighbor." The patient replies, "Thank you. I will feel much better." This absurd drama is played a million times a day in psychic illness, but few see it. A sufferer always thinks he will feel better if only his wife or boss changes. But the wise man realizes that medicine can heal the patient only if taken by the patient.

Bruce J. was one of those who wanted nothing more to do with the old and unworkable ways of his past years. He was tired of paying the price for his own wrong assumptions. But he wondered what to do with the many confusions he still faced, which brought the answer, "Never fear confusion. Live in the very center of it, without fighting or resenting it. Do this and see what happens." Something entirely new happened to Bruce.

The confusion in people regarding helplessness must be cleared up. To realize personal helplessness is the beginning of both true wisdom and new life. It is never shameful to be helpless. Do you know people with a public show of confidence who weep in secret? They need this lesson. However, at the same time helplessness is realized, there must be no feeling of hopelessness. Let there be another part of us which is encouraged over our honesty, just as we honestly admit we don't know how to speak French as our first step in learning French.

Small groups of people meeting together can help each other along the way. They can meet regularly, perhaps once a week, at the home or office of one of the members. The leader can read a paragraph or two from an instructive book and then lead the discussion. One group in California found it interesting and beneficial for each member to bring a specific question or problem to class for discussion.

Alex G., a business consultant, asked, "How might we summarize our purpose in attending these classes?" Reply: "People accept their unhappy lives as a child accepts a fairy tale, complete with ghosts and dragons. So living under the unconscious authority of fairy tales which are taken as realities, they have no alternative but to fear and fight. You are seeking the alternative which exists in reality."

PRACTICE SELF-OBSERVATION EVERY DAY

Self-observation is a classical technique which leads to self-liberty. You should observe your thoughts and words and acts impartially, reacting with neither praise nor condemnation to whatever is observed. You must not identify with anything, that is, you must not think that your thoughts and acts represent your true self. Self-observation enables you to separate yourself from mechanical thoughts to become more conscious and happy.

Because people fail to understand, they object, "But what if everyone spent their energies in self-study? How would we feed the hungry and heal the victims of war?'' The answer is, if everyone spent their energies in self-study there would be no hunger and no victims of war. These tragedies are the precise results of non-study, of human hypnosis. How few really see the appalling waste of human productiveness in self-war which explodes into international war. The first thing a man must do is the last thing he will do, which is to take an honest look at himself.

Suppose a lawyer takes you for a drive to show you all the property you have just inherited. The lawyer himself is a wealthy man with considerable property in the same neighborhood as yours, however, he discusses nothing but your inheritance. This illustrates why the truth is so appealing. It does not talk about riches out of our reach, but shows us what is our very own. A new consciousness reveals our rich inheritance.

Many people are puzzled when told they must become conscious and aware human beings. What does it mean to be conscious? Nothing mysterious. It means to see things as they really are, and not according to personal preference, imagination, or borrowed ideas. Man's chief barrier to consciousness is his delusion that he is already conscious. The crumbling of this delusion is the first task of whoever wants out of the trap.

Robert B., a student of esoteric mind-power, came to say, ''I am now aware of some of my false ideas about life, but they have terrible persistence. Part of me insists upon retaining them. What can help me here?'' Robert was told, ''Any time you think of how painful it might be to live without illusions, think how painful it is to live with them.''

Everything we are talking about is good news. There is nothing that is not good news! It is good news to hear that you need no longer endure the old ways. The idea of self-elevation through self-insight is good news, as is the classic principle of finding ourselves by first losing ourselves. It is fascinating news as well as good news to realize there is nothing at all wrong with being a failure in human standards of success and failure. As you proceed, you will produce your own good news.

Imagine a merchant from a distant land who displays some rare gems to prospective purchasers. Because the gems are found only in his land, they are viewed with suspicion. That is the same reaction given to teachers of truth. Man, living by artificiality, can neither understand nor accept the genuine. Realizing this, the teachers invite, "Examine, investigate, experiment, and sooner or later you will see for yourself what a great treasure is here."

HOW TO START TOWARD A NEW LIFE

In the days of sailing vessels, a cargo ship dropped anchor off an unknown island in the West Indies. The captain sent a dozen sailors in different directions to explore the land. As each man reported back, the captain added the fresh information until he finally had a complete map of the island. Valuable self-mapping proceeds like this, so turn yourself loose to explore every corner of your own nature. Consciousness of whatever is there is what makes you the captain of whatever is there.

Remember that all psychological chains are unseen, unconscious. That is why they *are* chains, because we are unaware of them. Knowledge of this prevents many mistakes. Ronald K. thought of forming a partnership with a new acquaintance. However, his study of human nature made him conscious of the fickleness and unreliability of many people, so he decided against involvement. It saved him trouble, for the other man later proved himself to be unreliable.

The way to do something is simply to start doing it. You don't need details about how to do it; just start. The way to think for yourself is to start thinking for yourself. The way to get rid of worry is to start understanding the false power of worry. The way to learn from unexpected events is to start listening to the valuable lesson they are trying to teach.

Of all the terms which describe man's difficulty, the term *self-defeating* is of maximum help. The aim of all the great teachers, like Christ and Buddha, was to awaken men to their self-defeating behavior. This phrase helps men to connect cause and effect, to see how their own negative thoughts produce disastrous consequences. This is a positive revelation, for a glimpse of self-defeating behavior *as* self-defeating always includes its opposite—a first glimpse of self-favoring ways.

Wallace T. commented, "People say they want to get out of the kindergarten of life, but what they really want is someone to repair their broken toys. I have become conscious of this synthetic sincerity in myself, and it's about time. I mention this because it may help someone who finds self-confrontation a difficult task. Believe me, there is no pleasure like the pleasure of tossing out useless toys."

Why are men and women satisfied with their manufactured amusements? Because their limited vision is never questioned. A man who has never seen a loaf will think a crumb is wonderful. A teacher who tries to exchange the man's crumb for a loaf must be willing to bear his hostility. The teacher's patiently presented message can be summarized in one word: "See!"

If a man will just see it! If only he will turn his vision inward to see how he has pasted dozens of labels onto himself and then called these labels "myself." A simple awareness of this would instantly remove the pains revolving around this fictitious self, including self-concern, self-confusion, self-guilt.

HOW TO DISCOVER THE TRUE

If you know that Ben Nevis is the highest mountain in Scotland, and your friend does not know it, your knowledge does not exist for your friend. This illustrates the task faced by those who have experienced the new life and try to tell others about it. It is easy to tell men about a physical mountain, but to describe an invisible world is another matter. So remember, our adventure is to see something which may not presently exist to our consciousness, but which can appear as the complete answer to life.

There need be no confusion over different terms used by various teachers, past or present, East or West. Simply see that they are all describing the same reality in their own words, like ten men would variously describe the same moon. Religious teachers refer to *God,* a philosopher speaks of *reason* or *naturalness,* a mystic talks about *Truth* or *Higher Power,* while a psychologist may prefer *reality* or *wholeness.* All describe the path to human rightness.

A ship trying to reach port found itself almost scraping the bottom of the channel. To lighten the ship, the captain ordered the crew to search out and get rid of anything useless below deck. The captain was shocked at how much junk came to light. Man rarely seeks out psychic junk unless forced to do so, and even then he carelessly mistakes it as valuable cargo. Even when weighted by suffering he twists it into strange kinds of pleasures. This is why the great teachers emphasize, "To discover the true, see the false as the false."

Several class-members wondered, "If human intelligence can build space ships which land on distant worlds, why can't we use our intelligence to end human chaos?" Answer: "Because space ships are built by mechanical thought, by memory, which has no power to understand human chaos. This is why you must sense the existence of higher thought, of consciousness and awareness. Aim at ending human chaos in your own human nature, which will explain everything else to you."

If you no longer know what to do, it is a very good place in which to find yourself. It means you are beginning to see that mechanical thinking cannot rise above its own limited level. People who angrily insist that they know what to do are still caught in an agonizing stage performance. So you are in a good place, which must be used correctly. Remain right where you are, not fighting the emptiness, not seeking relief from anxiety. Just stay in your place and let it tell you something extraordinary, which it will.

Remember, this is a totally new way, so leave memory and imagination and preference behind. Do not describe a new scene you may meet, but keep your mind entirely free to receive the description coming from the scene itself. If a vacation tour takes you through unfamiliar country, you do not assume that a distant lake is the same lake you have back home; you suspend assumptions in favor of unfolding facts. This is what we must now do.

WHY THESE TEACHINGS
ARE UNIQUELY HELPFUL

Ordinary teachings for man's deliverance make a great error from the very start. They are unaware of the deep confusions and self-deceptions existing in man. These methods urge people to live a life of love, but self-deluded man can only pretend to love. They urge men to work for a better society, but since man cannot create anything higher than his own low level of understanding, society never really gets any better. The teachings of this book are entirely different. Like good doctors, they know the cure because they first understand the ailment.

Society's systems for salvation can only add a new burden on top of an old burden. Man's overwhelmed mind has no idea of what to do with all the social schemes thrust upon him, but his desperation forces him to try to make sense out of nonsense. And in spite of all his elations and all his hopes, he knows he is no better off than he was before. The aim of these principles is to free the mind of its own net, to show us how to go beyond man-made schemes about life to dynamic life itself.

There is a great difference between false principles and truthful principles which should make you gasp with delight. Whoever sees it is no longer content to remain his own prisoner. False principles may be flattering and dramatic, but they have secret contempt for human capacities; they don't believe in you. Truthful principles give you full credit for natural intelligence. Knowing that you are able to escape, they provide aid and encouragement for succeeding.

There is a way by which you can have life entirely on your own terms. This way cannot be possessed by the self-divided man, for not really knowing what he wants from life, his demands change from day to day. But when you are undivided, when you are one with yourself and one with everything else, there is no separation between you and whatever comes your way. In this state, your terms and the terms of reality are the very same, making conflict impossible and peace permanent.

Swiss philosopher Henri Frederic Amiel had an interesting adventure in the Alps which parallels our inner discoveries and delights. Ascending a steep path to the Sparrenhorn peak, he recorded, "I could study the different zones, one above another—fields, woods, grassy Alps, bare rock and snow, and the principal types of mountains." Taking in a vastness he had not known before, Amiel exclaimed, "How great is one's reward!"

ABSORB THIS SUMMARY OF CHAPTER 1

1. It is totally unnecessary to live with daily frustrations.
2. Seek the truly practical—and you will surely find it.
3. It is a right move to honestly doubt your present ways.
4. Accept the invitation to healing offered by these ideas.
5. Group meetings are a valuable aid to self-enrichment.
6. Practice the technique of sincere self-observation.
7. Our wise task is to abolish self-defeating attitudes.
8. Consider yourself to be adventuring toward higher life.
9. Have confidence in the unique power of these principles.
10. Start today with this completely new way of living.

Chapter 2

HOW TO CHANGE INTO A
TOTALLY NEW PERSON

In order to attend the meeting, Irwin F. had turned his afternoon office duties over to his assistant. "I have driven for three hours," he said, "to hear a single point explained. You say we must bluntly ask ourselves questions we don't want to ask. May I hear one such question?" Reply: "You have a certain pattern of life. What has this pattern produced? Happiness? Patience? Understanding? If you have not received these, does it make any sense to remain in the pattern?"

If you will go through enough shocks you will come to understanding. A first shock is to see that human organizations set up for mankind's spiritual benefit can do nothing for mankind. A second shock is to see that you must search alone. A third shock is to see that you do not know what to do. A fourth shock is to realize that anxious efforts to know what to do only increase the confusion. A fifth shock is awareness that a battling self cannot create a peaceful self—and now you are getting close.

All you need to know at the start is to know that you want something much different and better than you now have. That is budding self-awakening. Maintain this wish. Never settle down with self-satisfaction. Remain dissatisfied with where you are, but never fight people and events which seem to block your progress. Study your dissatisfaction carefully, remembering that progress means just one thing: An increasing understanding of yourself and your life.

People are always eager to know whether there is a new way to change their lives. Of course there is, but it must be *new*, not merely *different*. We don't find the new way by accepting a different doctrine or teacher, for that only changes the exterior scenery. We find the new way by getting so tired of the old way that we are willing to give it up. With that, newness begins.

It is difficult for people to understand the idea of total self-change. When urged toward self-transformation they think it means to be more polite or to drop bad habits or to gain a broader education. But this is like changing a book's cover while thinking it supplies new contents. This barrier can be broken by remembering the first two steps in genuine self-change: 1. A man observes himself as he really is, which is different from how he imagines himself to be. 2. He permits the revelations to do their own good work of dissolving his imaginary self, which makes room for something entirely new and creative.

You don't have to ask permission from anyone in order to transform yourself. It is your life. Don't hand it over to others. Don't ask, "Is it right to go against everything I have been taught up to now?" Say instead, "Let me see how much intensity I can put into my search!" Your own wish for freedom is the only search-warrant you need.

VITAL FACTS ABOUT YOUR TRUE LIFE

From birth onward, a man collects hundreds of ideas about himself as being good or bad, wise or stupid, confident or fearful, and so on. Through repetition, these false identities harden into what he calls "I." It is this "I" which tyrannizes his life, but he cannot see it because he has never explored himself. But as he understands the process, he willingly gives up his false sense of self, to begin a new and true life.

It is not a disaster to discover that you are not the person you assumed you were. To the contrary, it is the beginning of the end of disaster. Experiment. How would you feel if you were *neither* a success nor a failure in life? How would you feel if you were *neither* popular nor unwanted? Can you conceive a way of life in which these opposing self-definitions do not exist? There is such a way, and it is the way of true life.

It is delightful to hear yourself exclaim, "Ah! I see what I am doing! I am abandoning a false sense of goodness in order to invite what is truly good for me. I am solving my problems by realizing that they exist because of my own false beliefs. I am living more vigorously by refusing to waste my energies in negative emotions. I am approaching authentic understanding by giving up what I used to assume was understanding."

The new way to see the world of people and events must begin with a new way of seeing ourselves. The outer world is a reproduction of our inner world. Realize this! How many troubled people do you know who have not given the slightest attention to this vital fact? Now you know why people remain in their blurred lives. How should you see yourself? As someone capable of self-enriching self-change.

Inward change is followed naturally by a change in one's speaking habits. A person can clearly notice this transformation as it takes place within himself. He finds himself speaking less impulsively and more consciously, that is, he is aware of what he says as he says it. He does not waste energy in useless talk, and he is not afraid to remain silent in certain situations, as many people are. As his level of being rises, so does the quality of his speech, just as a growing tree produces higher apples.

"I see the folly of rejecting an idea just because it is unfamiliar," said Bob F., "but some false ideas are also unfamiliar. How can we avoid falling into the trap of a new but wrong idea?" Answer: "Withhold conclusions. Don't accept or reject a new idea. The truth is like a voice you cannot identify at first. If you suspend judgment while

listening alertly, something in you will know whether the
voice is that of a friend or of a stranger.''

The illustration of man as a psychic prisoner is a helpful one. Let's examine one special feature of it. In an actual
prison, the guard has the key, and so, the prisoner cannot
get out on his own. There is a difference in a psychic prison,
which will stagger a man who first suspects it. In psychic
prison, the prisoner himself has the key in his very cell, but
is unaware of it. We need not plead with anyone for the
key we want; we have our own.

THE GREAT ADVANTAGE YOU POSSESS

Henry David Thoreau remarked that it took him only
a week to wear a path from his cabin to Walden Pond. He
was illustrating how quickly our beloved habits make us
dull. Most people live in a series of sour disappointments,
broken only by an occasional spoonful of sugar. What a
tragedy to feel that this is the best we can do with our
lives. We are not confined to the habitual path. ''I may
be thinking incorrectly toward myself and my life.'' A man
begins to change when this exciting idea begins to melt his
frozen beliefs.

Alertness provides those fascinating first glimpses of
how different things can be. Our world is changing because
we are changing. Looking inward, we find ourselves suddenly
wondering why our mind saw another person as inexcusably
rude, when it could have just as easily seen him as a lonely
and terrified human being. Looking outward, we see a husband in a moment of playful affection toward his wife,
which happens, we know, because of his moment of psychic
spontaneity.

If you do things in a new way, you will win a new life. For
example, never try to relieve the pressure of an embarrassment. Do not explain or plead or apologize. If you do, you
will not understand your embarrassment. This means its
cause will remain within you, to pop up again and again.
Embarrassment is destroyed by watchfully enduring it.

If you want to bake a cake you must have the flour
and sugar and other ingredients. If you cannot locate one
of the essential items your success as a cake baker is
stalled. If you feel blocked in making a better life, look for
a missing ingredient. Perhaps you have not shown enough
patience with yourself. Maybe you mistake a change in
feeling or circumstance as a change in your level of understanding.

In order to see what it means to be awake, we must
first see what it means to be asleep. We are asleep if we
suffer, are confused, if we experience conflict, inner and
outer. To see our actual sleep is not as easy as it seems.
You cannot make a man understand something when his
bank account or his sex impulse feels better by not understanding it. When a man begins to see what conflict does
to *him*, self-awakening is near, for no awakened man punishes himself.

Spencer W. said he had been seeking relief from his raging
aches for the last five years. He had tried various religions,
psychiatry, had attended self-help meetings, but nothing
worked. "My search started," he explained, "when I caught
glimpses of the awful aches inside me. For years I thought
I had everything, but now I see I have nothing. Wasn't I
better off when living in my daydreams?" Reply: "Is a man
walking toward a ditch better off because he walks in his
sleep? Nothing beneficial can ever happen to a man until
he sees something about himself he never saw before. What
has happened to you may be shocking, but it is right; it is
the only way out of your aches."

The great terror of the unawakened man is his painful
inability to understand what is happening to him. He feels
like a soldier caught between his fear of the battlefield and
his captain's command to attack. But his plight is not at all
hopeless. He can start right where he is to distinguish between the true and the false. A great advantage is his from
the very start, for there is an instrument within him which
already knows the difference. The piano is there; it just needs
tuning.

THE RICH DISCOVERIES
OF MARCUS AURELIUS

The reason a home is so comfortable is because it contains everything necessary for our changing needs. The reason we feel so uncomfortable when absent from our psychic home is because our true needs are not supplied There is no supply of love and gentleness and conscience outside of our real residence; we seek in vain if we think so. Human beings plod through life like drowsy camels, never suspecting what could be theirs if only they would turn homeward.

People say they wish to be intelligent and peaceful and honest. All right. There is a way to become these virtues and many more. All a person needs to do is say, "There are many things about myself I do not understand, therefore, I will make an earnest and a persistent effort to study my own nature." If the person really means it, nice things will happen.

"I would like to be a self-aware woman," said Anita H., "but I cannot understand what I must do. Is it really that mysterious?" Reply: "It is not mysterious at all. When the waiter sets your dinner before you, do not lose yourself to its pleasant sight, instead, be aware of your reactions to its arrival. Others at the table will not do this, but you can do it. You will feel something different. This awareness is the very same awareness which makes you a problem-free woman."

There is great healing power behind the classical teaching: "Watch!" It is found in the New Testament, among the Sufis, in the books of the East, and elsewhere. "Watch what takes place when you set aside your habitual ideas to listen to the new. Watch your mind's operations with quiet interest. Watch what happens by placing naturalness before an invented identity."

Realizing the need for earnest effort, a study group in New York agreed upon these rules: 1. If the truth wishes to expose our weaknesses, we let it do so without protest. 2. We wish to be strong in fact, not in mere appearance.

28

3. We do not place a limit on our powers of understanding.
4. We will not accept difficulties as an excuse for procrastination. 5. We wish to become the free men and women we are capable of becoming.

"You need only receive what is freely offered" is a fundamental teaching of higher thought. Knowledge of what it means to receive is a long leap ahead. To receive and to understand are the same thing. To understand is to receive. The receiving of a glass of water is intimately connected with the understanding that water quenches thirst. Think of receiving life-good like this, for it inspires the quest for higher understanding.

Emperor and philosopher Marcus Aurelius was a living example of an eagerly receptive mind. He supplied a long list of what he learned from his teachers, which can be summarized: From Sextus: how to dwell in harmony with nature. From Severus: how to love the truth. From Apollonius: how to remain steadfast in rightness. From Rusticus: how to avoid doing good for the sake of public applause. From Diognetus: how to distinguish truth from superstition. From Fronto: how to observe the wrongness of envy. From Maximus: how to live in self-government.

THE PURPOSE OF TRUTH IS TO HELP

Gilbert E. had first tasted esoteric truths when he accompanied a friend to a class. Impressed by the direct usefulness of what he heard, his personal interest developed rapidly. His first comment in class was, "I am afraid I am tense toward some of these ideas. Even though I know better, I feel as if they are against me." Comment: "I know, but we must not be impatient with the truth. Regardless of how we see it, the truth comes with the single purpose of helping us."

The truth is warm, kindly, healthy. It is something you feel independent of friends and environment; you know it all by yourself. The truth inspires because it connects what is real in you with what is real in the universe. The truth is all you really need because it includes everything you really need, which you can know by experience. The truth inspires because it is the truth.

Men will not receive higher truths because they feel endangered by them. The slightest threat to an established position is met with suspicion and antagonism. The passage from error to truth is solid ground all the way, but hypnotized man imagines himself to be treading a shaky bridge. How can he snap out of his nervous hypnosis? By remaining with one foot outstretched for even a short time, he will feel for himself the solidity of the ground touched by his foot. His first success in permitting reality to win over imagination will make him eager for more success.

The true hero goes forward without setting up requirements. Ten men applied to be explorers of a distant land. One declared, "I cannot go until you guarantee a soft bed." Another stated, "Count me out unless I can bring my wife." A third announced, "I will go only if I am made a leader." Only one of them said, "I will go," and he was hired on the spot.

The way a man presently behaves is the only way he can behave presently. His behavior is determined by his psychic level; he cannot act above that level, for he *is* that level. Then how does a man uplift his behavior? When realizing that a hawk or a sheep *must* behave according to its own nature, something awakens in him. He begins to see that only a total transformation of his deeper and secret nature can make him new.

You can tell a man ten thousand times that he had better find another way for himself, but nothing will happen until he *tells himself* this very thing. This point is reached when his suffering becomes unendurable, when he has run out of hiding places, when he will gladly exchange his pretenses for realities. This point is frightening at first, for he senses that he must now leave behind everything familiar and comfortable, to journey toward a gigantic question mark. But his decision is correct, he is on the right path, and questions will become answers as he bravely proceeds.

If you place a piece of metal near a magnet, the magnet

takes over with its drawing power. You cannot see the power itself, but you can definitely observe its results. If, regardless of how wrong we have been in the past, we will place ourselves near the source of rightness, the power of rightness will do the rest.

WHY YOU SHOULD BE DELIGHTED

A teacher summarized his teachings to his class: "You can escape the terror of your present life and win a new life. To do this, you must be aware of your illusions. To do this, you must observe yourself carefully. To do this, you must be humbly honest. To do this, you must want a new life more than your present life. And that is that."

The right way exists. The right way is known. Then where do we go wrong? Imagine a long stretch of railroad tracks leading from a dry desert to a mountain home. The tracks themselves are safe and reliable. However, at one point a tree has fallen across them. At other places the tracks are blocked by fallen rocks and roaming sheep. Just clear the tracks of whatever does not belong there and you are on the way. Just clear the mind of whatever has no right to be there and you have a clear track home.

A motorist heading north is free of the road hazards to the south. This introduces an idea of endless delight. By traveling in the right spiritual direction, there is so much nonsense you can ignore! It is in back of you, out of sight and mind. What kind of nonsense? What about the foolishness of human quarrels? What about the tiring folly of putting up with childish people? Think of some nonsense you would like in back of you, then be delighted at your ability to put it there.

A member of a study group asked, "How does a teacher know which inquirers are sincere and which are not?" Reply: "While he knows at a glance, he does not need to do anything; the inquirers do everything by themselves. A truly hungry man does not permit anything to stand in his way of obtaining food. A man who merely pretends to have spiritual hunger goes away at the slightest so-called insult to his inflated opinions about himself.''

To see that we do not know is the beginning of knowing. It is a healthy surprise to see that we do not really understand that which we have so forcefully talked about so many times. We dislike to admit lack of knowledge, for we fear it would endanger our psychological security. But we fail to see that our reluctance does the very opposite of what we expect. Instead of providing security, it keeps us insecure, for it keeps us in psychological darkness. To see that we do not know is itself a ray of light.

If we wish the earth to produce a flower, we must first bring a seed to the earth. If we wish to produce truth, we must first bring something to it which is already a part of truth, for nothing foreign can enter its kingdom. So bring your intense interest, bring your weariness with your usual life, bring your desire to understand what life is truly all about.

Edgar Q. said he had searched both Europe and Asia for the cure to his dissatisfaction. ''I am firmly convinced of the existence of something totally different,'' he avowed, ''but at the same time a stubborn part of me will not consent to self-change. What can I do?'' Reply: ''You may not consent to the battle for self-conquest at first, but you can consent to being made consenting. This serves as the heroic soldier who rallies faint-hearted comrades around him to form a solid and effective army of liberation.''

HOW TO AWAKEN TO A NEW LIFE

What kind of man possesses possibilities for self-awakening? He is the man who feels, even dimly, that he is living under some sort of a gigantic hoax. He has observed the senselessness of his life, he has noticed how people are really quite ruthless beneath their masks of decency. This is a crisis for the man, for now he must decide whether to start thinking for himself or to dazedly endure the horrible hoax. It is a crisis, but also a fresh chance. What man who feels himself caught in a hoax wants to remain in it?

Learn the difference between exoteric and esoteric religion. Exoteric religion emphasizes church-attendance, either heavenly or earthly rewards, good works in public, the labeling of oneself as a believer, and so on. Esoteric religion emphasizes sincere self-examination, a desire to abolish pretense, a willingness to do without public recognition, an effort to understand the meaning of life, and so on. Which do most people prefer? Which can make a man real?

You don't have to have a reputation for being a good person or a religious person. You just need a deep conviction that nothing matters except to live in naturalness and simplicity. That alone makes you a good and religious person in the true meaning of those words. Then you will see with delightful surprise that goodness truly is its own reward. You will then not be a public moralist, but have the private peace of one who has found the truth at last.

You must dare to disassociate yourself from those who would delay your inner journey. Yes, it takes daring, for you are leaving the familiar but the wrong, the comfortable but the hypnotic. Others will not want you to make the journey and may even employ pressures and threats, for you are menacing their own hypnosis which they love so much. Leave, depart, if not physically, then mentally. Go your own way, quietly, undramatically, and venture toward trueness at last.

Practice at placing the spiritual before the material. First attempts may reveal how seldom we do this, which is a healthy surprise. When applying for employment, your first aim should be self-command, not the desire to make a good impression. When speaking with others, your goal should be to speak with self-awareness, not to persuade others. The only important thing you have to do with your life is to make it a right life. Use this method for making it right.

How clear it all becomes! Randolph Y. had searched diligently for the true meaning of mercy. He did this, he explained, because he felt the need for mercy himself. He finally realized that mercy never comes from some mysterious and remote being in the sky, nor from another person, but comes through his own awakened mind. Mercy is the same as the ending of unconscious self-punishment, which comes by loving truth more than illusion. We show mercy to ourselves by replacing our earthly nature with our cosmic nature. This is what became refreshingly clear to Randolph

START CHANGING YOURSELF RIGHT NOW

As I write this book I can glance up through the window to watch the gray and tan chipmunks avail themselves of the food and water set out for them. One chipmunk turned into a comedian by climbing inside half a cantaloupe and rocking back and forth while nibbling at the fruit. The rocking motion was no doubt unusual for a chipmunk, but he bravely endured it in order to eat the fruit. Our first taste of new truth may cause unusual psychic motions, but our endurance satisfies psychic hunger. Later, we look back and smilingly wonder what we were so worried about.

Nothing you *really* need is out of your reach, but the very reaching produces a false belief in the need to reach out and secure something. You are never divided from what you really need, which may not be seen as yet, for you may not realize your own present self-completion. Be aware of your reaching. Be aware of how it never reaches anywhere, but is always dissatisfied. Be aware of how tired you are of it all. Now you are making it!

"What attracted me to higher teachings," remarked Helen E. at a group meeting, "was their ability to understand everything about me. They seemed to know me intimately, like a friend. At first I was disturbed by what they knew, but then I had a second reaction—their power of understanding may be matched by their power of assistance. That was exactly the case. I have a way to go, but I am on the way."

One sign of psychic growth is the increasing realization that an authentic teacher knows more than we originally thought he knew. He knew it all the time, but we had no way of discerning his wisdom until we acquired the same wisdom in ourselves. You can stand on the sidewalk and look up at someone who is enjoying the view from the top of the building, but you do not know what he sees. When you climb to his height, you see what he sees.

The act of changing our nature into a truly rich nature is an interesting process in itself. Years ago, scientists gazed out at the vast oceans of the world and wondered whether it might be possible to convert salty sea water into fresh water for man's needs. They learned how to do it and they did it. If you wonder whether you can change yourself, just go ahead and do it. Even when you say, "I want to learn more about the inner kingdom," you are already brightening something.

TEN OUTSTANDING POINTS IN REVIEW

1. Let self-development start with self-knowledge.
2. Your own permission is all you need for life-transformation.
3. These truths create delightful feelings of rightness.
4. As we elevate our thoughts, we elevate our world.
5. Never place a limit on your powers for advancement.
6. The purpose of truth is to heal and to inspire.
7. We must clear the mind of its habitual obstacles.
8. Be rewarded by having an intense interest in these ideas.
9. With diligent search, everything becomes clear at last.
10. You are never separated from your authentic needs.

Chapter 3

WIN DAILY SUCCESS IN HUMAN RELATIONS

The wise man always sees human nature as it is in fact, not as it appears to be on the surface. We see this healthy honesty in the stinging plays of Henrik Ibsen, in the blunt epigrams of La Rochefoucauld, and in the rebuking sermons of Jesus and Buddha. A negative fact about human nature can be changed, but nothing can be done with a pretty illusion except to suffer from it. Place a rose over a wound and you still have a wound.

Whenever you cannot understand why your relations with others are so inharmonious, return to this lesson: When you are an expert on yourself, you are also an expert on everything else. An eagle knows itself, it knows its own nature, therefore, it knows everything about other eagles who have the same nature. Know yourself as you are and you will know others as they are, which makes you very wise in your human contacts.

Self-awakening is speeded up by clearly observing the human scene in all its chaos and heartache. George Mac-Donald describes the pathetic picture, "There they go— little sparrows of the human world, chattering eagerly, darting on every crumb and seed of supposed advantage!" To see how bad it really is does not indicate a negative personality, but reveals an honest mind. And it can arouse the declaration, "I refuse to live like that!"

Michael J., a factory foreman, used his daily human contacts to learn more about human nature. Each day he wrote down a single fact he had observed. Here are three of his conclusions: 1. Everyone is far more frightened than he appears to be on the surface. 2. People gain a false and self-destructive feeling of power by hurting others. 3. Strength based in authentic wisdom is the only foundation for right human relationships.

It is not wrong to detect falseness in others as long as we look with equal vigor at ourselves. In fact, it is health-therapy at its best to see in ourselves what we see in others and to see in others what we see within our own system. For example, notice how people twist words to serve their personal interests, as humorously admitted by a sign in a shop: "We buy junk and sell antiques."

If you fight against the established system, you are part of the established system. If you are part of the system, you are attacked by it. If attacked by it, you are really attacked by unseen negativities within yourself, so fighting the system is like giving ammunition to the enemy. Stop fighting the system, which is pointless, and start fighting for yourself, which makes sense.

"How can the human race stop quarreling?" asked one class member. "If we could just find a system for ending our quarrels!" Reply: "You don't need a system for ending a quarrel; you just stop quarreling. Quarreling humans pretend to believe in a system, such as peace conferences, in order to continue quarreling while appearing peaceful. Systems are avoidance of immediate sanity. Sanity is now, not tomorrow."

HOW TO BE AT EASE WITH EVERYONE

The only thing on earth which protects a man from the wrongness of others is freedom from his own wrongness. Self-error and other-error occupy the same level, so collision is inevitable. But to see one's own wrongness is an unpleasant shock to self-invented self-pictures of being a right person, so few pass through this test on the path to liberty. To see our own reluctance to shatter false images is a fine step in the right direction.

Hardened concepts prevent self-rescue. Socrates once gazed in wonder at some statues of human figures which had been skillfully carved from stone. ''What equal skill men have,'' he reflected, ''for turning themselves into stone.'' Self-melting and self-recovery are the same process. How involved are you in your own self-transformation? Inquire into it.

Asked Bruce M., ''How does the abandonment of a false sense of self establish true relationship between people?'' Response: ''Please follow carefully. I cannot see myself as *I* unless I create you as *you*! I see myself only by contrast to you. Therefore, I deliberately create you as either a friend or enemy in order to—so I falsely think—establish myself as a labeled *I*. However, this identification of myself as an opposite to you is false from the very start, for only oneness is real. When I see this, both illusory friends and enemies disappear, leaving me in true relationship with everyone.''

All the great thinkers taught Oneness. They showed that man is One with God, the universe, and with himself. Illusory thinking makes man believe that he possesses a separate and individual ego which must be expanded and protected. This illusion causes wars and every other human misery. When an individual realizes his Oneness, his personal conflict ends completely and forever.

We like in others what we like in ourselves; we reject in others what we reject in ourselves. We are therefore attracted or repelled only by our own alternating self-images, while mistakenly believing that others cause our feelings. This is practical self-knowledge. By abolishing both self-praise and self-condemnation, and thus thinking from a higher level, we are never falsely fascinated by others, and therefore never hurt by them.

When you are in charge of yourself you are also in charge of everyone you meet, but in a totally different way than most people think. You are placed in charge by not needing to have charge over anyone. This is natural, non-neurotic, peaceful power. This remarkable psychic state belongs to whoever has achieved, in the words of Eastern teachers, "Obedience to the nature of things."

Can you imagine yourself being completely at ease with everyone you meet—completely at ease? This calmness can be yours whether you meet the president of a country, or someone who knows your secret past, or a hostile person. Nervousness is caused by permitting past experiences to impose themselves upon the present moment. The claim of the past upon the present is illegal, which you must detect as illegal. Stand on the bank of the Mississippi River and look at it. A minute later you still label it the Mississippi River, but the flow before you is new. Can you see in this the secret of ease?

YOUR NEW KIND OF VICTORY

To understand why human affairs happen as they do, we must deeply examine human nature as it is. No other investigation makes sense, though people who are hiding something will try to offer substitutes, such as forming "peace committees." The tireless investigator of human nature understands and becomes immune to human malice. For example, you can tell how viciously a person will persecute others if he gets a chance by noticing how viciously he screams when he himself is persecuted.

"Why," asked Bill W., "are spiritual teachers so emphatically against all kinds of social schemes which are supposed to bring greater human harmony?" Reply: "Because people who get sick from drinking impure water cannot get well by drinking more impure water. Human schemes can never cure human illness, but few see it. The reason medicine cures illness is because it is different from illness. Your work with these principles is showing you the difference between impurities and medicine."

George Gurdjieff, a teacher of esotericism, used to conduct experiments which revealed the shocking difference between a man's professed ideals and his actual inner emptiness. Someone with very strong opinions would be put into a psychic state which temporarily blocked out his surface personality. When asked whether he still wanted to give his forceful opinions, the man would stare dully around and say he had no interest in them whatsoever—all he wanted was some raspberry jam! "Strip away false personality," concluded Gurdjieff, "and you find a small child who is very fond of sweets."

During a discussion about the superior insight of spiritually awakened men, the following was said to the class: "Would you like to meet a man who knows all about you at a glance? Some of you are smiling. Most people would hesitate to meet a man who sees instantly through human pretense, yet he is the only one who can provide authentic aid. Understanding the illness, he also understands the cure. But the patient must want to get well."

An awakened man has a unique relationship with society. He is like a spectator at a football match who knows all about the game but who does not play himself. Having risen above the disastrous error of taking sides, he is unconcerned with winning or losing. It is his deep insight into the game which makes him valuable to those who are tired of the kind of winning which soon turns to losing. He shows them a totally new kind of winning, which is not a contest, but an undivided path.

What makes our human relations whatever they are? We are attracted to whatever we already are. By contacting other minds similar to his own mind, a man becomes more of what he already is. The taste of the honey is determined by the kind of blossoms visited by the bee. Whoever fails to work on his inner self is mechanically attracted to more of the tasteless life of aimless society. Whoever first works alone on himself acquires a taste for consciousness, which attracts him to other conscious people.

VALUABLE PRINCIPLES FOR HUMAN HARMONY

Lloyd F. requested, "Please explain how self-work frees

us from troublesome people.'' Reply: ''Remember that bickering and antagonism supply a false feeling of life to many people. They use quarrels as a fiery stimulant, just as others use alcohol or drugs. They can't live without agitation. Such people unconsciously and persistently seek out human relationships which they sense must result in conflict. After getting their thrill, they depart to seek another fight. To answer your question, if you are above this level, you do not attract such people, for you do not have what they seek.''

Most people, when faced by a resentful person, either get resentful themselves or try to lower the other person's resentment by appeasing him. Both responses are wrong. The wise individual will try to understand why he permits the other person's resentment to dictate these responses. Then he should firmly reject them. With this, the other person's problem of resentment remains where it should remain—with the only person who can solve it, which is himself.

Never do favors for others so that they will be pleased with you or in order to get them on your side. These are false moves which incur penalties. For one thing, others will sense your need of them and will scornfully take advantage of you, while pretending friendship. Also, such acts increase the false belief that strength resides in others, rather than in yourself. Be an independent nation which refuses to trade with treacherous countries.

Be your own keeper and you can forget the irritating question, ''Am I my brother's keeper?'' The self-responsible man who has climbed to the top of the mountain for himself does not guiltily feel he owes anything to those who insist upon remaining on the prairie. Begin at once to see a feeling of guilt as just another psychic tyrant you must overthrow.

Don't make another man's problem your problem. If someone behaves badly toward you, why be disturbed? People have such false guilt about everything that they actually feel obligated to get upset over another man's upset.

Your duty is to save yourself; his duty is to save himself. Wisdom saves, not sentimentality.

A false sense of self adds the load of a false sense of responsibility, which then adds guilt that one is not living up to his "moral standards." Another illusion in this dynamite factory is the illusion that one can actually do good to others. This accounts for the endless production of senseless social schemes and organized drives for "a better world." Emerson declared, "Society never advances. It recedes as fast on one side as it gains on the other." Only individual consciousness can uplift anything.

A man who *is* good does not go around *contriving* to do good. His own goodness does good, wherever he goes, though few realize it. Being one with goodness, he has no separate self-image of being a good man who can help the bad to be good. He leaves such imaginary and ego-centered goodness to the self-deceived. The bad man *thinks about* goodness with personal gain in mind, while the truly good man impersonally *expresses* goodness. Because a rose *is* a rose, it never needs to think of itself as one.

LET PATIENT SELF-WORK TRANSFORM YOU

When dealing with others, and you don't know whether they are right or wrong about something, observe them alertly. Notice whether they reveal negative traits, perhaps suppressed hostility or self-praise or subtle accusation. You know that negativity can never be right, which means their position is also wrong. There are no faulty signs without a faulty sign painter. Put yourself to the same test with equal alertness, for it builds rightness.

An understanding of human hostility is helpful. Hostility is a frantic attempt to throw up a wall between the individual and some truth about himself he fears to face. But hostility cannot protect because it exists within the man himself. Hostility as a weapon of defense is like a foolish man who attempts to burn down his enemy's house, but in the darkness burns his own.

Do not see the badness or weakness of others as being necessary to them. Give them the same opportunity for self-awakening you have given to yourself. This does not mean sentimentality toward them, nor the attributing of non-existent sincerity to them. It means to see them as frightened and confused human beings who can, by turning around, save themselves from themselves. This helps you break down the false division which the words "you" and "I" seem to create. Also, it is psychic law that whatever gentleness you give to others you also give to yourself.

Awareness shines like a light in the night. What is the condition of an unaware man? He does not know that he does not know. He is unaware, and so he is unaware that he is unaware. And being lost, he gullibly gives other lost people an opportunity to make him even more lost. Do you know anyone in this condition? Somewhere along the line—and right here is the best place—that man must exclaim, "Enough of this nonsense!" Already, his awareness has changed his direction.

The man who needs to be accepted by others still lives under several wrong impressions. He still thinks there is value in self-pleasing human associations and in reassuring words which come from people who appear self-assured. He still thinks he can escape the agony of his own emptiness by filling it with the neurotic noise of society. The awakened man has no attachment to the opposite terms of "acceptance" and "rejection." Living above mere words, he comes and goes among people in a quiet contentment which is unknown by those who still seek acceptance.

Al H., a pharmacist, wanted to know how his own level of psychic maturity affected his relations with others. The information included, "Weakness is always sensed by others and it is always exploited. Can you see the connection between your own supposed needs and the way others treat you?" Al later reported, "I am no longer going to need the company of certain people. It costs too much. I am not hostile toward them; I just have a fresh view of things."

You want to come back and they won't let you? That's

all right. Something went wrong and you no longer have
your former comfort and security? You may not understand'
as yet, but it makes no difference. Just think on these
higher ideas, just work patiently on. You will see for yourself that it is all right and always was. Then you will not
want to come back.

THE STRANGE VALUE OF SELF-SHOCKING

The happy life with other people exists when they are
volunteers to your company. Promises of reward or threats
of punishment can only create slaves who will revolt at
the first opportunity. Society is slavery. Mr. A. submits to
the tyranny of Mr. B., only on the condition that Mr. A. will
have his turn at dictating to Mr. C. You should let people
come or go as they please, just as if it makes no difference
to you. It makes no difference, which is not coldness, as
others will think, but love, which they will not understand.

"In your last lecture," said Dean W., "you spoke of the
falsity of trying to impress others. In the few minutes we
have left, will you please review the main points?" Reply:
"What is wrong with *not* being impressive? Have you
ever asked yourself that question? There is nothing wrong
with it, but frantic people use impressive appearances to
distract themselves from the very problems they complain
about. The need to impress others causes half the world's
woes. Don't add to them. Be real, not impressive."

In human affairs, there are really no such things as superior men, mediocre men, or inferior men. These are mere
labels which men apply in a vain attempt to feel superior
and to avoid the feared inferior. All unawakened men occupy the same unhappy level. So-called superior mayors and
colonels and executives are just as secretly afraid of life
as so-called inferior ones. To see this aids our abandonment
of the flat prairies of human thought in favor of the peaks
of esoteric insight.

The reason great social nonsense is so hard to see is
just because it is great nonsense. We can admit the petty

nonsense of wearing uncomfortable clothing in order to appear respectable, but beyond that sort of thing men halt in apprehension. Men refuse to see the danger of hero-worship for fear it would shockingly deprive them of one of their most reliable escapes from self-emptiness. There is something they do not know: Any fact is valuable to the degree of its ability to shock the individual who faces it.

If we can find ways to bear the shock of seeing ourselves as we truly are, half the battle is won, for this is where most people come to a halt in their homeward journey. The following facts will aid and encourage anyone: 1. The shock is simply a dynamic part of the healing treatment. 2. It is the only way to pass beyond self-confusion. 3. It is true heroism to bear the shock. 4. It is never harmful, always beneficial. 5. A bit of endurance increases strength for more endurance. 6. It is the right thing to do for yourself.

We can add to our essence, which is beneficial, or we can add to our surface personality, which only snags things all the more. How can we tell the difference? Our inner nature knows the difference quite clearly, so we must be alert to its signals. Whoever yields his mind to attractive charlatans will add to his own false behavior. Whoever bears a truth he does not want to hear will add to his essence.

Realize the enormous value of simply starting. The very first effort to understand an idea is like a bugle call which brings your various energies together into a united force. Something within you exclaims, "Well! So it can be done after all!" Remember, the way of liberation is not complicated in itself. If we listen we hear, if we hear we learn, if we learn we grow, if we grow we succeed.

CONSTANTLY OBSERVE HUMAN NATURE

When self-work creates self-understanding, we neither like nor dislike other people in the usual meaning of these terms. If we like them, there is always the possibility of the opposite attitude arising, consisting of dislike, perhaps after a quarrel. But self-understanding includes other-understanding, which is above these opposites, which is authentic love.

We must hold no bitterness toward those who shatter our dreams or delay our expectations. Bitterness indicates an absence of the true view toward whatever happened. Liberation from this painful feeling can be illustrated by a man who hopes to find a promised reward behind a grape vine. When not finding it, he turns bitter, but upon wise reflection he realizes it was the grapes he was hungry for after all.

See the difference in believing in another person's badness and in understanding it. This works for your own development. Getting disturbed over another's badness means we have not as yet seen through the bluff of badness; we still wrongly attribute power to it. Sometimes when observing destructive human behavior we react, "How pathetic," instead of, "How wicked." When this contains no dramatic sentimentality, it is the beginning of understanding and compassion.

Ted C. stated, "You have said that consciousness is the same as wisdom. What is an example of this in human relations?" Reply: "The conscious person detects what the mechanical thinker never notices. Have you ever watched someone behave falsely while knowing he could not detect his own falseness? Consciousness of rightness quickly detects whatever is unlike that rightness. You can see the daily value of this, especially when dealing with unreliable people."

The next time you are with a group of people, perform an experiment. Do not speak, except in brief reply, but quietly observe the surrounding behavior. Notice how people fear silence, listen as they anxiously describe the important and wonderful activities in their lives. Observe that man who speaks so loudly and confidently, and see a frightened sheep who acts brave because of the temporary absence of the wolf. This insight into human desperation is part of your journey out of it.

If there was nothing else wrong with living in psychic sleep, its dangers should be enough to shock people awake. A man in such sleep is like a dull-minded visitor at a zoo who thinks the iron bars are to keep him from harming the lions. How can a man in such peril from himself work to end his danger? He can connect his own ways of thinking with the mauling he gets from life.

After awhile, we begin to see the reason for things. We see why negative emotions must be understood and removed —because they punish the very possessor of them. We realize the importance of turning our attention toward the inner world—because that is where we really live, for either peace or sorrow. We see why facts must chase out beliefs—because only facts can heal the wounds caused by shaky beliefs.

YOU NEED NOT EXPLAIN
YOURSELF TO OTHERS

Abandon all concern with public appearances. The weariest slaves are those who anxiously wonder, "How will I appear to others?" Attention to appearances blocks attention to where it should be—with the building of authenticity. A man thinks he is obligated to appear intelligent and so never thinks of his real obligation to be intelligent. What would you pay for a life in which you did not have to explain yourself to anyone? That is the kind of life we are talking about.

Myron V. asked, "Will you please summarize the idea that other people cannot really control me?" Summary: "The reason no one can really control you is because you do not exist in the sense you think you do. You are not your cluster of memorized ideas about yourself. Awareness of this dissolves both the cluster and the belief that others can control you. If you have a self-image of being a desirable person, others can control you by flattering it, but what can they control if you have no such image?"

Human beings live by echoes, and when hearing none they get scared. A man invents certain ideas about himself—as being pleasant or dynamic or popular—and then broadcasts these ideas to the surrounding world. While preferring an agreeable echo from others, he will also accept a critical one, for nothing terrifies him more than complete silence. We must learn to live without echoes, for that is true living in which there is no fearful dependency.

People yearn to be near to others without having the slightest idea of what it means to be near. Nearness does not mean physical closeness, nor does it mean domestic or social organization. And nearness definitely does not mean the sharing of a mutual desire, for wolves can share the desire to destroy a sheep. This is separation, masquerading as nearness. Only a free mind can come near, for it has broken its own walls. It has a friendly message for others who are breaking their own walls.

A lost traveler follows his rescuer out of the desert, even if the traveler wonders at the directions taken by the rescuer. Our similar task is to follow the facts wherever they lead, resisting nothing, fearing nothing. We must alertly guard against our fixed preferences, which is accomplished by remembering that they delivered us to desolation in the first place. Follow this thought all the way: Who but you knows your inner state, so who but you can change it?

At the start of your search it is perfectly natural to meet the unexpected. Sometimes, instead of finding clues, you are surprised to uncover new puzzles. This is not only normal, but perfectly healthy. Do you see why? Because it is good, never bad, to become conscious of far more confusion than we thought we had. Why is this good? Because consciousness is health, now and forever.

GUIDES TO GREATER HUMAN HARMONY

1. The wise person is a constant student of human nature.
2. We understand others as we understand ourselves.
3. These principles will make you at ease with everyone.
4. Our inner state attracts people on its own psychic level.
5. You are never responsible for irresponsible people.

6. Self-insight supplies skill in handling other people.
7. Experiment with the practical techniques in this chapter.
8. Do not be shocked by human weakness, but understand it.
9. Be quietly unconcerned with what others think of you.
10. The conscious man cannot be controlled by others.

Chapter 4

THE COSMIC SCIENCE OF LASTING HAPPINESS

Here is a question submitted in writing during a class session: "We seem to have the potentialities for happiness, but have none of the happiness itself. What is wrong?" Response: "A wild bird imprisoned in a cage still possesses its capacities for natural happiness, but cannot use them. Likewise, we possess natural capacities which are blocked by unnatural psychic imprisonment. As shocking as it may be, admit your actual confinement. This defeats self-complacency and arouses a drive for naturalness."

All human neurosis and unhappiness consists of an unnecessary contradiction of life-energy. It is the pull of inner forces in opposing directions, with the person caught between. It is like a boatman cruising down a powerful stream, who periodically chooses to force his boat into shallow streams, only to find their attractions faded and himself grounded. If we would stick to the main stream of the pure psychic self, no such painful decisions would be necessary.

To understand the true nature of happiness it is needful to see what happiness is not. *What is usually called happiness is only a temporary distraction from unhappiness.* So all distractions from ourselves, such as noisy ambitions, are cunning forms of unhappiness. There is no such self-separation in genuine happiness, instead, we are always present to ourselves, content with our own company.

"It may be quite possible that I am living in an imaginary happiness," commented Dwight J., "which should be detected at once. How can I test myself?" Answer: "There are dozens of tests. Does your happiness depend upon exterior support? Do you feel contradictions and repressions within? Are you compelled to defend and prove yourself? Do you worry over the loss of what you call your happiness? Detect these, which is excellent self-work."

A child might think he could dwell in the clouds if only he could reach this or that hilltop. But upon reaching the heights he is disappointed to find the clouds still above him. This is the error of those who seek happiness outside of the here and now, but they seldom see it as an error. Their wild hopes play a hypnotic tune in front of their logic. You are after true logic. True logic, which remains in the here and now, possesses a delightful characteristic: It knows that facts—no matter how frightening they may appear to be—are always on your side.

When words like "success" and "happiness" are pronounced they activate our acquired definitions of them, which may be quite wrong. So our task is to be conscious of these mechanical interpretations and to deny them entrance. If I see that the word "happiness" is merely a sound made by holding my tongue and lips in a certain way, already I have detached myself from mechanical definitions. At the end of definitions is happiness as a fact. It comes because my memorized ideas about happiness no longer block the fullness of the unlabeled present moment.

HOW TO CHANGE DISTRESS INTO HAPPINESS

"I know how people stubbornly refuse their own rescue," said Edwin W., "because I fought it myself for many years. But will you please shed some light on why a man deliberately rejects what he needs to know?" Response: "He rejects knowledge because it is a threat to his self-image of being a man who already knows, who already understands himself. Do you see how self-images, while appearing to

give a man individuality, actually keep him among the confused crowds?''

Suppose you are asked to attend an important meeting.
However, instead of attending personally, you send a photograph of yourself. That photograph is lifeless, unintelligent,
incapable of understanding anything or of acting rightly.
This is exactly what happens when we send imaginary ideas
about ourselves into the world. This is why people fight
and agonize—for no other reason than that they attend life
with unconscious self-photographs which they take as realities. Whoever will see this can dismiss his images; he is
then personally present in every situation, which is handled
rightly with original intelligence.

Socrates commented, ''Slanderers do not hurt me because they do not hit me.'' Socrates had succeeded in doing
what we are aiming for in these pages, which is to get
rid of the bundle of anxious ideas we call ''I.'' If I have no
unconscious self-image of being an important and successful person, can I be hurt if called a failure? Of course not.
If I do not imagine myself as a worthy and a lovable person, can I be distressed if you leave me? No. This is what
happiness is.

''Many of us forget what we must do,'' said Wayne W.
''How can we remember to work on a solution?'' Answer:
''Remember the problem and it will help you remember
the solution. Remember that man's single greatest problem
is his clinging to a false sense of self. That helps you to remember that the solution is to see through and dissolve the
false self.''

What must you do to be saved? You find yourself by
abandoning yourself—abandoning what you unconsciously
call yourself. When dark feelings of despair and desolation
reach their peak, you are face to face with this unique opportunity. We are called to abandon our well-rehearsed
social roles, we are called to become real men and women.
William Makepeace Thackeray sums it up in the last line
of Vanity Fair: ''Come, children, let us shut up the box and
the puppets, for our play is played out.''

A teacher asked his students, "Have you ever noticed how people are chained by the very things they call their happiness? A woman is chained by her marriage, a man by his compulsive ambition, a schemer by his own deceptions, a famous person by fear of losing his fame. Have you ever noticed this?" The students gave this deep thought, and so should we.

Freedom from unhappiness passes through three stages: 1. Unconscious unhappiness, in which pain is felt but not understood. 2. Conscious unhappiness, in which a man becomes aware of his actual agony. 3. The ending of unhappiness, in which a full awareness of self-conflict has dissolved pain. Study each of these steps with careful attention, then open yourself to the life-changing experiences they will arouse.

A STARTLING FACT ABOUT SELF-PROTECTION

Nothing need make you unhappy. There is no need for anyone to be caught by unpleasant feelings. The way in which we get caught can be illustrated by a passenger in a car traveling a narrow jungle road. By carelessly dangling his arm outside the window, he is certain to be struck and scratched by the branches he passes. By keeping ourselves within awareness, within what is truly right, we keep ourselves untouched and unharmed.

Evelyn B. asked, "What can I do about my unhappy marriage?" She was told, "Realize that a hurtful marriage is not a separate problem. It connects with human thinking in dozens of ways, for instance, it is useless to demand that others behave according to our personal wishes. When you see that your own mental clearness is the perfect solution, you will work in the right place, which is your own mind. Then, self-correction automatically corrects exterior areas, including human relationships."

Happiness is never found in the opposite of a present state. The shy person assumes that happiness exists in bold action, the city man thinks it can be found in the country. No matter how often a man wins an opposite state he never sees the sameness of his inner nature. Happiness resides in the mind which does not divide life into opposites of any kind, including today and tomorrow, security and insecurity. Give this idea special consideration.

A conscious man is protected at all times, but his protection is utterly unlike anything known by a sleeping man. It is the protection of having no protection at all. If you protect anything, perhaps your reputation, it means you are protecting a human label, a mere word, which causes tension toward whatever threatens the label. So this kind of protection protects nothing; it just makes you nervous. But if you have no reputation at all—which is a wonderful way to live—there is no need for protection and there is no nervousness, for you are yourself only.

Do not let words block your understanding. Words are like paint. A piece of lumber can be painted blue or green, which conceals its natural color. If you say the lumber is blue or green, you tend to forget its concealed nature. To avoid this mistake in life, always see the original fact about anything, then, if necessary, you can describe it with a word. Place the fact first, never its description. This prevents self-deception, for it keeps the word true to the fact. For example, to justify anger is to paint it falsely. Human error can be corrected only when we do not cover it with colorful words.

We must be careful to not interpret positive words wrongly. Liberation does not mean escape from an exterior problem; it means insight into the inner cause of the outer effect. Love is not attachment to someone who provides a sense of security; it is a purified inner state which has no anxious craving for so-called security.

Unhappiness is set before the mind as dry firewood, but the igniting flame is not provided. So at this point we can choose to let it remain dry firewood or we can choose to light it. The harmless thought occurs, "I am alone," but anguish flares up only with the addition of, "I am therefore lonely." Catch thoughts at their entrance and keep them dry.

HOW TO WIN AUTHENTIC SUCCESS IN LIFE

A class member spoke up, "We often hear that man dwells in psychic sleep and spiritual hypnosis. Please review these descriptions." Response: "They describe the unhappy state of a man who does not live in tune with reality, and who does not know that he habitually substitutes imagination for reality. A man sleeping in his bed at night does not know he is asleep. He knows he was asleep only when he awakens."

Love and intelligence and goodness reside in the hypnotized person just as much as in the awakened man, for "the kingdom of heaven is within." But only the awakened man can enjoy them. If you don't find a lost picnic basket you can't enjoy it. The idea of simply enjoying their awakened nature rarely occurs to anyone. It comes to whoever finally sees that he need not spend his life trying to get something from someone else.

You love rightly when you love rightness. It is no more complicated than that. A father who truly loves his son will say to him, "Intelligently and efficiently earn your own living as best you can and have no concern whether society judges you a success or a failure. I don't care two cents whether or not you are a financial success—I just want you to be a decent human being."

When feeling unsuccessful in the eyes of others, you should ask, "Where did I first get my ideas about success and failure? Obviously, from other people. Now, people are terribly confused about life in general, so it seems likely that their notions about success and failure are also without meaning. Maybe I am the unconscious victim of mere words, of false values, of human delusions. Maybe failure and success are both utterly false concepts which torture me because I fail to see them as false. Starting today, I will investigate until I uncover the whole truth."

We will see how awareness turns us in the right direction. When a man wins a particular success in the world, he is never quite sure as to what he has just won. All he knows is a temporary escape from the anxiety which spurred his race for success in the first place. Suppose a man paused to consider this strange state of affairs? What if he saw that success was merely his idea about success, which vanished upon attainment of his goal? That would be a healthy surprise, for he would see through the illusory game he cannot win and which perpetuates the very anxiety he wishes to end.

People without these cosmic principles cannot possibly win authentic success in life. Do you see why? *They are not doing anything for themselves.* While it is just fine to engage in business and have a circle of friends, such activities can contribute nothing to the invisible man within. Until this is seen, nothing changes. When it is seen, everything changes. Whoever comes to this insight will truly succeed in life, for he now loves something which is above his usual interests.

YOU ARE NOT TIED TO SOCIETY'S FEARS

A manufacturer planned a business trip to Brazil. He asked an assistant to collect and submit to him some facts about Brazil which would make his trip a prosperous one. He studied the submitted information, but with bewilderment, for it failed to make sense. Investigation revealed that the assistant had mistakenly prepared information about Argentina, not Brazil. The point is, we must never accept information about life which does not make sense to our deeper sense of rightness. What we receive must be in accord with our true needs.

You must not believe what the social atmosphere is trying to tell you. Everyone and everything around a man is telling him that he must be afraid, that he must fight, that he must feel under pressure. Don't believe it for one second. Don't take their word for it. They do not know. You are not tied to the social atmosphere in any way. You are free of it at this very instant.

When we see the useless *as* useless, it falls away, just as we casually discard a worn-out coat. Roland J. saw the uselessness of arguing his way through life, which had been his habitual and painful way. This motivated him to search for the higher path, which he finally found. Roland had heeded the advice of Henry David Thoreau, "What is the use of going right over the old track again? . . . .You must make tracks into the unknown."

A man with an exterior cause is an unhappy man. His public enthusiasm cannot deceive his private nature. Regardless of how worthwhile his cause may appear to be in the eyes of others, it is his prison. It is a frantic but vain effort to escape the unescapable—self-confrontation. There is only one satisfying cause in life, which is the release of ourselves from all that binds. This true cause starts with receptivity, for when receptivity meets truth, something happens.

A few of us were sitting around the hall when Diane S. commented, "I am especially grateful for one particular point in your talk. You said that happiness can be described as a state of *absence*. That rang a bell. Contentment is an absence of a nagging need to be appreciated by others. Peace exists when we have no nervous desire to appear successful in the eyes of society. I am greatly relieved by seeing this. Thank you."

Your exterior life can be descending into what society calls failure, while at the same time your interior life is winning true success. It is your alert watchfulness of how exterior failure tries to depress your interior state which supplies this new kind of success. So-called failure need not wash over and soak your psychic system. A rightly functioning mind has no such problem. People aften ask, "What does it mean to be a truly wise human being?" This is it. The wise individual uses his exterior affairs— whether labeled a success or a failure—to build interior fortunes.

Never fear uncertainty. There is never anything to fear in uncertainty. Fear arises because men want to be certain

according to their own terms, but their terms are all
wrong. It is quite possible to have a thousand uncertainties
and not have a single fear. A cloud has no concern with
where the wind carries it; one place in the sky is as good
as another.

WHERE THE CURE FOR UNHAPPINESS BEGINS

People complain, "He made me unhappy," and "She
tore me apart emotionally." The only way to get rid of
these self-punishing attitudes is to ponder day and night upon this simple fact: When you bump your knee against a
chair, the pain occurs because of what happens in the
knee, not what happens in the chair.

You do not know that you are unhappy unless you tell
yourself that you are. A thousand voices inform you of personal unhappiness and all of them are wrong, for they
speak from the false idea of self-division. This means that
they separate you from the here and now, creating the illusion of lack, of unhappiness. One voice reminds you of
younger days, another deceptively promises happiness in
tomorrow, a third hints at fulfillment in exciting surroundings. Do not unconsciously tell yourself you are unhappy and you will not be unhappy.

An anxious young fish swam over to ask his father, "I
have heard of the ocean, but cannot find it. What and
where is the ocean?" His father replied, "Stop distracting
yourself with worry about the ocean and you will find it."
We are, in truth, already One with the universe and with
ourselves, but an anxious mind prevents self-realization.

"I want to be good company to my family," said
Mary C., "but daily irritations overpower me. Must it remain like this?" Reply: "What kind of company are you
to yourself?" That is the vital question. There is absolutely
no difference between your treatment of yourself and your
treatment of others. Because physical bodies are different,
you wrongly assume that you treat yourself different from
others, which is impossible. This is the one fact you must

grasp, for then you will begin the cure where it must begin—
within yourself.''

The runner who arrives first at the finish line wins the
medal. Your awareness may seem to have swift competi-
tors, like impatience or numbness, but none are as swift as
awareness. Discover for yourself the practical application of
this lesson. The next time you are tempted to feel lonely,
outrun it with, ''There is never anything wrong with being unnoticed and unwanted.'' If you are confused about a
problem, overtake the confusion with, ''A united mind,
which can be mine, solves every problem of a divided
mind.''

Unhappiness is caused by comparison. You feel unhappy only when you unconsciously compare your present
state with another state, perhaps when you were younger
or healthier, or perhaps when you had a certain compan-
ion or possessed certain public honors. Where there is no
comparison, unhappiness is impossible. Happiness exists
when the mind does not move away from itself, when it remains in the present time zone, when it declines to contrast
itself with another time or another condition.

We respond to life according to our psychological level.
The higher the level the broader the view and therefore
the better the response. A man living on the level of jealousy looks out and sees hundreds of younger or richer or
handsomer people who arouse his jealousy. A man on a
higher level looks out and sees so much heartache and
cruelty that a refusal to contribute to it arises within him.
To lift our level is to lift our happiness, for we *are* our level.

HOW TO THINK IN A NEW WAY

Imagine an unhappy man seated at home. The walls
are covered with paintings of various scenes. Stating, ''I
want to change my life,'' he gets up and changes the paintings for new ones. But when returning to his chair, he
finds himself just as unhappy as before. He changes the

paintings several times, but feels no change in himself. Do you know people who believe they can change their level of happiness by changing their exterior scenery? Where have they erred? How can they correct themselves?

The mind becomes panicky when it meets a problem it cannot solve. In its anxiety to relieve the tension it turns toward a false solution which just creates another panicky situation. So the mind's owner travels in an endless circle of despair. There is a way to end it. First, the man must dare to see that his usual kind of thinking can only make things worse. Next, he can realize the existence of a totally new way of thinking. Finally he can follow esoteric principles which will accurately guide him out of his circle of panic.

Gus D. requested, "May we have an example of what you mean by thinking in a new way?" Reply: "Instead of thinking about contributing something worthwhile to society, which is a totally meaningless idea, think about giving up wrong items within yourself. Very few will do this, for it is much easier to preach about service to mankind than to give up hidden self-deceptions which injure mankind."

People are confused and unhappy because they never know from one moment to the next which side they should be on. Nervously jumping back and forth like a caged canary, a man is haunted by fear of making the wrong or the less-advantageous choice. The mistake is the mistake always made by a divided mind—it thinks its life depends upon a secure attachment to either *this* or *that*. The single mind has no fear of either *this* or *that*, for it does not wrongly divide life into opposites in the first place. Being whole, it sees the whole.

Boredom is the result of building the same old castles in the sand, day after day. While sensing they cannot stand, people build them anyway, not knowing what else to do with themselves. Spiritual renewal is never boring; it is increasingly enthralling each day. What is more enthralling than to know you are on the way at last?

Hope, so highly prized by many, has neither value nor

meaning to the truly happy man. Examine this for your-self. See how hope creates *you* and an *objective,* causing painful self-splitting. So, strangely, hope produces the very feelings of hopelessness one seeks to avoid. Also see how it causes fear of nonattainment. The man without hope is self-unified, and so can never feel hopeless! Self-completion has no more need for hope than a healthy plum tree needs to hope for plums.

This is the only practical way. Which is more practical—to struggle to win someone over to your way of thinking or to have no need at all for struggle? Which is more use-ful—to tensely seek success when even the word has no real meaning to you—or to change your entire concept of what it means to succeed in life? Which is more important—to cling to a memorized religious belief or to be comfortable with your own company?

AN INVITATION TO THE RICHER LIFE

Learn this great secret of life: What people call interrup-tion or disturbance to their routine is just as much a part of living as the routine. To split life into two parts, one called routine and the other called interruption, is to be caught between them. It is the false sense of self with its anxious craving for so-called security which wrongly di-vides life like this. Dissolve the false sense of self and you will have a life which is neither routine nor disturbing, but which is whole.

A boat racer sought entrance to an annual contest held at a mountain lake. A judge explained to him that the boat did not qualify for entrance because of its many safety ha-zards. "There are too many differences between your boat and our safety requirements," said the judge," then in-vited, "why not make things right and try us again?" The corrected boat was added to the race. It is the many differ-ences between our ways and the ways of reality which bar our participation in the richer life, but correction invites en-trance.

"More and more," commented Gordon W., "I see how abandonment of the false makes room for the true. Please mention a false idea we should banish." Reply: "Banish the notion that attracting other people to you can make you happier or make you less anxious. Attracting another person can bring financial profit or marriage or an exciting evening, but it cannot uplift your consciousness, which is the only basis of happiness."

When a man receives praise or rewards, he replies unconsciously and silently, "Thank you for telling me who I am. I was worried about my identity until you affirmed it." Then, when the crowds drift away, in creeps the emptiness he thought he had escaped. At this point he can either give way to depression, or he can begin to see his error, which opens the way for something far beyond his usual sense of self.

Do not call yourself names of any kind. Permit no labels, not even so-called positive ones. Do not call yourself either weak or strong, foolish or wise. Dare to have no idea at all as to what you are and who you are. This may seem like a strange course to take, but remember, you want out of the human jungle, and this is the way out. Names and labels occupy a lower level of thought, the level of nervousness, which is not for you.

George MacDonald was a British author of novels with mystical and esoteric meanings. In one instance he tells of the father who accidentally dropped his daughter's watch. Undisturbed, the daughter said that as long as it was done by her father it was perfectly alright. This parallels our situation. As we understand our Oneness with a Higher Mind, everything is perfectly alright.

BASIC FACTS ABOUT TRUE HAPPINESS

1. To see what happiness is, first see what it is not.
2. Do not settle for imaginary peace, as do most people.
3. Happiness exists only in the present, not in the future.

4. Self-rightness is its own lasting contentment.
5. The self-aware man can never be made unhappy by others.
6. Study the lessons about words in this chapter.
7. Never accept the gloomy attitudes of unhappy people.
8. Have a cheerful receptivity toward truthful ideas.
9. The happy man is good company to himself.
10. Resolve to think in a new and triumphant way.

Chapter 5

TESTED TECHNIQUES FOR
MORE MENTAL POWER

Asoka, an emperor in ancient India, was one monarch whose private life matched the principles he preached in public. Asoka had the pure teachings of Buddha inscribed in public places throughout his kingdom. Wherever his people traveled, they were reminded that only a noble personal life has any value in this world. The same reminder comes to us from the pure teachings we inscribe in our minds.

Learn the difference between *thinking* and *awareness*. Thinking connects with the past, with memory, and works by opposites, such as good and bad, you and I. It is rightly used in everyday matters, such as cooking. It is wrongly used when one tries to gain a self-identity, like labeling oneself a success or a failure. Awareness is an impartial observation of the whole of life. It does not proceed from a sense of individuality; it is the whole tree, not just branches which are opposed to roots. Awareness is sanity, peace.

Would you like something to challenge and strengthen your mental forces? At the next disappointing event, reflect, "This is also just as much a part of life as what I label a favorable event. As a whole person, I see both sides equally; I do not split events into good and bad. Being whole, I see the whole." Do this, even if you don't understand it, for it contains a tremendous secret.

Rosemary J. smiled as she said, "You described me

perfectly when you said that most people change their minds as often as they change their clothes. I think I know what is right, but new opinions from other people make me doubt.'' Comment: ''The day will come when no one will be able to make you doubt what is truly right, for your own awakened wisdom will judge accurately. The same wisdom also exposes falseness which masquerades as trueness. You will be like a skilled fisherman whose quick glance toward his net shows him the difference between good fish and useless fish.''

Daily observation proves how seldom people really know the difference between right and wrong for themselves or for others. This is because they live by man-made rules, and when these rules inevitably break down, so do the people. How few human beings live from their own recovered essence, which alone is good and true. Live from yourself and you will have no problem deciding between right and wrong. Only the self-divided must make painful choices. A carnation never chooses because it never tries to prove it is a lily.

We use the mind to heal the mind, which comes by detecting and removing whatever is worthless. The reason we must look within is because we must seek help where it exists. To seek outside ourselves is to come back with the feeling we have been nowhere. Even if puzzling at times, it is delightful to see what we can do for ourselves. It is like searching around a tall building for a space rocket, only to suddenly realize that the building itself is the rocket.

FIRST STEPS TOWARD NEW MIND-POWER

What about mental prison bars? People have bars of regret over hurting others, bars of fear of self-facing, bars of worry over chaos in the world. Think of these bars as paper. They have no more power to hold you than paper. Ten thousand bars are still ten thousand bars of paper. But you must work to understand this, which is exactly what you are now doing.

A wise man was asked by an inquirer, "Why am I afraid?" Replied the wise man, "Because you have fixed notions." The inquirer then asked, "Why do I have fixed notions?" to which his teacher replied, "Because you are afraid." When our frozen minds melt in the warm light of understanding, there is a mental flowing in which there is no fear.

At a certain point in self-development, a new way of thinking appears. Mental and emotional disturbances are no longer seen as enemies which must be battled, but simply as wrong processes which must be corrected. This comes as refreshing relief, which is followed by an eagerness for deeper healing. The individual becomes increasingly willing to give up shallow values for the riches he senses lie just ahead. He is like Queen Isabella, who sold her personal jewels to make it possible for Columbus to discover the New World.

Clarence V., an executive in a plastics company, was eager to know more. As a member of a study group, he was given a specific task. He was to list three ways in which anyone could reverse his attitudes from negative to positive, and so unshackle his mind. Clarence reported, "I can try to understand a humiliation instead of resenting it. I can refuse the dishonesty of wishing revenge while calling it justice. I can dare to live without tormenting thoughts which give me a false feeling of existence."

Begin to reverse your thinking. Do you think human happiness can rise without a rise in human consciousness? Reverse that thinking. Do you believe in the necessity of personal conflict? Believe it no more. Do you assume that self-security and self-protection require you to sacrifice yourself to others? Reverse that idea once and for all.

A dozen mysteries are solved when a man understands what is meant by mechanical thinking. Now seeing that mechanical thought cannot rise above itself, any more than an automobile can fly, he knows why he failed in former attempts at self-change. His new insight into the limits of mechanical thought is accompanied by knowledge of the full power of conscious thought. At this point his self-work is more and more taken over by universal forces which work through him and for him.

Interrupt the mental films which hound you. First, be aware of how often your mind unreels unpleasant or distressing scenes based on past mistakes or sorrows. Awareness of their presence is essential, otherwise, you cannot take the next step, which is to deliberately interrupt them, to break off their mechanical action. If you feel a small shock at the interruption, you are doing it rightly. This is one of the finest favors you can do for yourself.

HOW TO THINK WISELY IN DAILY AFFAIRS

By shaking a compass you make its needle swing around to any number of wrong directions.When you stop agitating it, the needle settles down to point toward its true and natural direction. Here is a lesson in mental control. We can practice a quiet refusal to accept agitation as normal and necessary. This is a settling process which points out the true course in every situation.

Rex E. came with the familiar question, "Why does my life unfold the way it does? I am always walking into trouble of one kind or another." Our walk through life is no mystery to the person with a thorough inner education. I discussed with Rex the law of cause and effect, trying to make him see that *his* causes produced *his* effects. He took with him the principle, "If your mind goes right, your walk goes right."

Whoever thinks inaccurately toward spiritual matters will also think incorrectly toward earthly affairs; he will fail to understand them. The spiritual does, in fact, command the material. So the only intelligent course is to seek first the kingdom of inner knowledge, after which wisdom and competence in earthly activities are added effortlessly.

The man of mental clarity sees the falseness of both human optimism and pessimism. Both are false emotional states which fail to see life as a flow of natural and impersonal events. The optimist feels the pleasant breeze of an event and thinks it is a reward for him exclusively. He turns into a pessimist when the next breeze blows pleasantly on his neighbor instead of on himself. The clear-minded man lives above both of these artificialities. He lives in a third state in which he is one with himself and therefore one with all events.

Said a student, 'I find it difficult to distinguish between what is right and what is wrong for me, but you say it is easy.'' Response: "How do you know that a smile is right and a scowl is wrong? An inner sense naturally tells you. Your natural knowledge about right and wrong in every area is presently lost because of cherished fairy tales. Give up fairy tales.''

An esoteric school is not a place; it is an alert mind. You can be profitably enrolled in school day and night, wherever you go. You are in school when you notice a slight change in the face of an apparently cheerful friend, which reveals his deep depression. Your schooling is proceeding nicely when you suddenly realize that the person who clings to a false idea is the same person who is punished by it. Unfortunately, this kind of school is not glamorous enough for many people. They want impressive teachers in saffron robes and incense filled chapels.

LET YOUR MIND SOAR FREELY

A man's life is determined by what he challenges or fails to challenge. Challenge the power of wrongness to masquerade as rightness and wrongness loses its power to deceive. Challenge fear and trembling before the unknown and you understand that the unknown is not separate from you and is therefore not a threat. Be an alert challenger.

Mr. and Mrs. Clyde W. said they were unsure whether their minds were working for them or against them. They wanted new information for making their minds favorable forces. They were helped by hearing,

"There is a simple test for determining whether or not we are thinking with self-benefit. If either an enemy or a friend appears to be exterior to us, we must reverse our mind. The enemy or friend is always within, though the mind projects them outward, thus deceiving us."

If you feel blocked and frustrated in your attempts to rise above yourself, return again and again to the following: The everyday mind we use in home and office cannot understand higher principles. Everyday thoughts are like birds confined to a cage in a zoo. They can fly so high but no higher. Our first realization of this is somewhat startling, for we mistakenly fear there may nothing above this limited height. But later our consciousness magically transcends the cage of everyday thoughts to soar freely in the vast space above.

Have no fear of launching out into the world of unknown ideas. There is nothing to fear. You don't have to know where you are going, in fact, to go rightly you must have no idea of where you are going. Don't try to guide your footsteps with an old lamp that has failed you a thousand times before. Say to yourself, "I may not know where I am going, but I do know one thing—I am not going back to the old ways." Say it explosively.

The part of the mind called memory can be compared with a news film taken fifty years ago. Viewing the film, you would not agree to live today in the uncomfortable ways of the past. Yet, this is exactly how man lives mentally, but fails to see it, which places him under the tyranny of time. People live today from yesterday's hardened ideas, for example, a man lives with unconscious guilt over past mistakes. An earnest inquirer will see his past cancelled completely. He will be as new as each new day.

Determine that your mind will not be taken away from you at various times throughout your day. That is just what happens when we fail to forbid negative thoughts. Negativities are like thieves who easily take what they want because the owner remains asleep. Let consciousness guard your mental home. Depressing or confusing thoughts cannot take away your natural tranquility as long as the mind is guarded by awareness.

Every once in awhile, take a key word regarding mind-power and review a helpful fact about it. If you select the word "intentions," you could say to yourself, "Earnest intentions are a strong ally in mind-building." Here are other key words to use: 1. Consciousness 2. Self-responsibility 3. Receptivity 4. Newness 5. Self-awakening.

WHAT IT MEANS TO BE CONSCIOUS

Man is like a clock with a face showing twelve o'clock, but which strikes the time of six. A mechanical clock cannot see its contradiction, and neither can man see his self-division while living from mechanical thought. A clock cannot heal its self-contradiction, but man can do so by conscious thought.

"Please define consciousness," someone requested, which brought the following reply: "Consciousness means to plainly see the facts about anything, without the interference of conditioned thought. Since conditioned thought always judges everything in its own favor, it is incapable of seeing a fact impartially; it uses a fact in an attempt to back up its own self-serving position. For example, a conscious man sees crime as a tragic consequence of human ignorance, while an unconscious man feels a secret superiority to criminals."

To *know about* the truth is not the same as being *one with* the truth. To *know about* is to have mental knowledge only, to be *one with* is to be the truth itself, with no separation between the knower and what is known. This healthy self-unity appears as a false sense of self falls away through self-insight. It would be profitable to study this idea in a class you may attend, or with interested friends.

An awakened mind has power to come right to the point about a human problem and solve it immediately. It has direct perception, similar to the straight flight of an airplane. This is a rich result of a deep desire to find out what life is all about. Buddha's clear mind came right to the point regarding human suffering, which he set down as the Four Noble Truths: 1. Sorrow exists. 2. Sorrow has a cause. 3. This cause can be ended. 4. There is a way to accomplish this ending.

Psychic hypnosis and harmful illogic go together, like two outcasts stumbling in the dark. For instance, people decline to face the facts about themselves, fearing their harshness, but they fail to see the harshness of living in untruth. The dozing mind is dull, repetitious, like water in a cup, while the awakened mind flows with sparkling originality every new moment, like a mountain brook. Our task is to go beyond the words which describe this experience to the experience itself.

A wounded man may jump a bit when the doctor touches the wound, but there is no fear or resentment toward the physician. The patient understands that the doctor has no hostile motives, does not wish to hurt him, but is simply advancing the cure. Healing comes swiftly to the spiritual patient who reaches this stage of understanding. Mental and emotional disturbances are no longer seen as enemies which must be battled, but simply as signs that something needs correction. This intelligent attitude opens the flow of healing, and sensing it, the patient opens himself to the flow until the cure is complete.

Harvey T. said, "After class last week, some of us were discussing mental maturity. How do you define a mature man?" Reply: "If you remember our studies about contradictions in man, you will see there can be only one definition. A mature man is one whose true exterior behavior is matched exactly and at the same time by true inner behavior."

HOW TO SEE LIFE IN A NEW WAY

Our objective is a full use of the mind. In addition to the powers of memory and recognition and enjoyment, we want to think with calmness, awareness, understanding.

To do otherwise is to be like a king who lives in only one small room of his spacious palace. Our new discoveries come through a courageous exploration of the mental castle. We achieve what we dare to achieve.

The study group was discussing various forms of fear, when Orville Q. remarked, "This class has helped me to get myself out into the open, which is great gain. So let me admit my fear of my life collapsing upon my head. You know what I mean. I have certain securities in my family and employment, but am nagged by fear of their sudden collapse." Orville and the class studied this brief but pointed reply: "There is no collapsing but the collapsing of wrong ideas. When you see this, the fear of collapse collapses completely."

Whenever you feel yourself falling from a position which you feel is secure or advantageous, let yourself fall altogether, without resistance. Do this watchfully, consciously, with a wish to learn something new. You will finally see that there is no difference between what you call advantage and what is called disadvantage. This is superior thinking—and great relief!

A man came to a famous lecturer and asked to be taught the art of eloquent public speaking. Accepted, his first three lessons consisted of nothing but sitting silently and restfully in a chair. When the student objected to the unusual procedure, his teacher explained, "A babbling mind must produce a babbling speech. I am teaching you the eloquence of a quiet mind."

Have no hesitation in taking daily mental vacations, which is something many people fear to do. They believe it is their own thoughts which hold their world together, when the precise opposite is true—their confused thoughts split their world wide open. Life lives itself in perfect wholeness, but to experience it we must dare to take mental vacations, regardless of the consequences. The consequences will be self-reconciliation, which comes after the self-daring.

The mind divides itself into opposites, producing opposing viewpoints, rival political parties, and so on. See that much clearly. Next, see how people select one side or the other in order to get a feeling of identity. Next, see how the taking of one side automatically creates the other side, thus producing quarrels, war and other tragedies. Finally, see that consciousness is a totally new way of seeing things. It sees both sides at once, but identifies with neither. This is a truly intelligent and compassionate state of mind.

Start out on this escape route: Don't take sides with your own opinions. This may seem incredible to you, which is just fine, for you are on an incredibly delightful journey. Don't identify with your opinions, don't take them as you, for they are not you any more than changeable leaves are the whole tree. This creates a new state in which you take sides with your natural intelligence, you are one with yourself.

BE AWARE OF YOUR PASSING THOUGHTS

The trouble with one wrong idea is that it leads to another. If we believe in the necessity of trying to win over others, we will also believe in the need for wearisome scheming. Fortunately, the process can be reversed by letting one right idea lead to another. By realizing that nervousness is caused by protecting false ideas, we can also realize that calmness comes by abandoning the false.

Imagine a roomful of tourists who have gathered to hear a lecture about Ceylon, one of the lands on their tour. While waiting for their guide, some of them scribble their ideas about Ceylon upon a blackboard. But the ideas are vague and contradictory, arousing good-humored arguments. Their guide enters, looks at the blackboard, erases everything, and writes down the facts. We cannot be reminded too often of the need for erasing the faulty to make room for the accurate.

Stand on the seashore and watch the ships sail by. There is no problem as long as you simply stand there and watch them. Only when you identify with the ships do you distress yourself. If you say, "This is *my* ship," you will grieve when it passes from sight. If you say, "*I* must command that ship," you arouse fear that someone else will become its captain. Likewise, by simply watching our passing thoughts, we prevent harmful identification with them. We cancel time, which means unconcern with the thought-ships of either yesterday or tomorrow.

Become acquainted with your mind by sitting quietly alone and watching it. Make no attempt at control; just let your mind think whatever it likes, with you as the alert observer. Such an alert person might see the flow of thoughts as, "Money . . . anxiety . . . dinner . . . comfort . . . hurry . . . sex . . . television . . . yesterday . . . desire . . . violence . . . watchfulness." This casual-but-alert obervation of your own thoughts is already a measure of release from negative thoughts which do so much harm.

When told they must not suppress their violent thoughts, but should become aware of them, people react in alarm. They worry, "But what evil might I do if taken over by violent thoughts?" This is misunderstanding at its worst. A man is a captive of violent thoughts precisely because they are unconscious. Further, he is already in the state of violence he fears will capture him. That is why humanity suffers from war and crime and cruelty. You can wave this fact as a red flag in front of people and they will still refuse to see it. But whoever embraces the fact will know what it means to live without suppressed violence.

A new student commented, "Sometimes I fear the explosions of my own mind. All of a sudden it screams." Response: "You should not be frightened in the least by these screams. Just be quietly aware of them. Remember above all that mental stability comes by examining the contents of the mind, not by avoidance. Most people avoid, but you need not make that mistake. Study your outbursts with calm interest, just as a scientist impartially studies objects under a microscope."

As an experiment in mental purification, let go of negative thought the moment it arises. Be aware of its appearance, then let it recede into the distance. A negative idea will fall away of itself every time unless it is held by giving it non-existent value. No harmful thought need remain in the mind any more than you need to keep worthless food in the refrigerator.

HOW TO ATTRACT BENEFICIAL CIRCUMSTANCES

It is quite true that we turn into whatever we constantly think and talk about. German philosopher Arthur Schopenhauer saw the negative side of this law. When dining out, Schopenhauer habituallly placed a gold coin on his table. When asked about his curious habit he replied, ''If I ever hear anyone in here talk about a truly worthwhile topic I will give the coin to charity.''

It helps to see the difference between mechanical thinking and conscious thinking. Mechanical thought moves horizontally, like a tractor on flat ground. Conscious thought moves vertically, like an automobile ascending a hill. Man-made plans for human betterment, like social schemes and moral preachings, change nothing, for they are purely mechanical. While giving a temporary appearance of newness, they soon prove to be another section of the same rocky ground. But conscious thinking by a sincere individual lifts him above the mechanical level, which frees him from the disasters suffered by those still on flat ground.

Marie J. inquired, ''How can I get rid of haunting thoughts, especially those connected with a shocking experience I once had?'' Response: ''The haunting persists because you give them false value. They provide fiery agitation, which you unconsciously prefer to the unknown state of a quiet mind. These hauntings connect with wrong ideas, for example, that others owe you something. Insight into this will dissolve haunting thoughts. Tear down the haunted house and the ghosts disappear.''

The mind attracts whatever is similar to itself. A frightened mind attracts frightening experiences. A hostile mind attracts other hostile minds. The operation proceeds under the same cosmic principle by which squirrels or ravens are attracted to their own kind. Our aim is to make negative people and unhappy events foreign to our mind, which elevates us to a new law. This new law attracts whatever is favorable to us.

A rightly functioning man can be compared with an efficient and orderly city. A city has many sections and services which contribute to the health and happiness of the whole population. It has residential areas, sections set aside for business, education, recreation and other necessities. Since they are intimately connected, the whole city benefits when each serves rightly in its own way. So does a man's wholeness depend upon a harmonious operation of all his areas. When the mind and the emotions and the body all agree, the man is whole.

SUCCESSFUL IDEAS ABOUT MIND-POWER

1. For daily benefit, deeply observe the ways of your mind.
2. Consciousness creates peace, aliveness, psychic health.
3. We must courageously abandon all fixed ideas and opinions.
4. Mechanical thought is limited, but consciousness is limitless.
5. Never accept mental and emotional agitation as necessary.
6. Study carefully the laws of cause and effect.
7. Gladly accept the unique lessons coming from fresh ideas.
8. To be conscious means to clearly see the facts of life.
9. Release negative thoughts the moment they appear.
'0. Nothing disturbs the man who controls his own mind.

Chapter 6

THE NEW WAY TO SOLVE PERSONAL
PROBLEMS

A puzzled seeker of ancient Persia journeyed for many months to seek an answer to his question, "Why does my life unfold the way it does? Why do I meet certain experiences and misfortunes?" He asked at every temple of wisdom along the way, until one wise man provided an answer that was both surprising and enlightening: "Wherever you go, you meet yourself."

An individual's primary problem is not defeat, inferiority, tiredness, alcoholism, danger, separation, regret, obscurity, indecision, shyness, melancholy, oppression, ridicule, poverty, rage, society, betrayal, disenchantment, weakness, or opposition. The individual's problem is unawareness of his personal immersion in the psychic hypnosis which commands mankind.

When society does not know what to do about a problem, it invents theories to make it appear that it does know what to do. The appointed crime committee concludes that crime is caused by poverty or drugs or broken homes, which is like saying that illness is caused by sickness. Social problems are caused by human ignorance of spiritual truths, but since few can face this fact in themselves, the problems continue.

A problem which is not met with higher principles will simply create another problem. It cannot happen otherwise, for problems exist on the mechanical level of

thought, and mechanicalness can only produce more mechanicalness. It is like a rock tumbling down a hillside
which strikes and activates other rocks. This explains why
some lives consist of one difficulty after another. Higher
thinking can turn such lives into one triumph after another.

Ruth L. habitually let her husband do the talking, but
during one afternoon class she seemed eager to express herself. She spoke up, "I think and think and think, but my
problems persist. Why?" Ruth heard, "Because thoughts
cannot rise above their own level. If you think it is necessary for you to endure the boredom and fatigue of going
along with unwanted social activities, that thought will pin
you down. Think higher. Think that you can live as you
want, which is a fact." Encouraged by hearing herself
speak out, Ruth took an increasingly active part in the discussions.

Whenever you are offered a cure for problems, ask
yourself, "Is this an authentic cure or is it just another distraction masquerading as a cure?" Your own excellence depends upon it. Remember, your wisest and most loyal friend
is your own deeper discernment. It is always on your side
in questions like this, but to release its power you must refuse attractive but empty bottles which are offered as medicine. Begin today to say "no" to anything which you sense
is contrary to what is right for *you*.

A VITAL QUESTION TO ASK YOURSELF

Bernard T. worked in a large office building which
brought him into contact with dozens of people every day.
"I see personal unhappiness all around," he stated, "but
you say we must examine our own conflict. This baffles me
because I don't see myself as having deep problems."
Reply: "Of course you don't, which is just why they are
so dangerous. You need to be shocked out of it, but only
you can give permission for this shock." Bernard nodded

and commented, "You say that most people dwell in dream-land, which no doubt includes me. All right, I give you permission to wake me up."

When a person mentions his problem, there is always a deeper problem beneath it. The wife who asks, "How can I make my husband more considerate?" also asks, "How can I banish my pain of feeling ignored?" People seldom mention the deeper problem, partly because they are unaware of it, and partly because they dislike admitting it. In your situations, proceed wisely by digging down to the deeper problem. When self-insight dissolves it, the surface situation ceases to exist as a disturbance to you.

Never ask, "What can I do with my problem?" In all the history of mankind, no one has ever found an answer to this question, for none exists. Always ask, "What can I do with myself?" One of the most persistent illusions of man is that human problems are somehow separate from human nature. That is like thinking that a cherry seed has no connection with a cherry. Ask, "What can I do with myself?" and you ask an honest question which attracts a lofty answer.

What do we truly need? What should we take and what must we leave alone? It is both a problem and yet no problem at all. It is like a woman in a grocery market who believes she has left her shopping list at home. Unable to remember her needs, she feels lost and bewildered. Suddenly, she remembers. Reaching into a pocket she had neglected to explore, she finds both her shopping guide and her confidence. When we remember what we have done with ourselves, we find our self-guide and our self-confidence.

Whenever you meet a problem or a crisis, take it completely upon your own shoulders. Do not try to share it with others, which cannot succeed anyway. If you dilute the intensity of the problem by spreading it around, you also dilute your power for understanding and removing it. Of course, this is the exact opposite of what everyone else does, but you no longer want to be as confused as everyone else, so you will do what is right for you. Solitary work returns the richest reward.

There may be times when a problem in finances or human relations seems like a mountain in comparison to the particle of truth you presently possess. Don't believe it; not for one second. Behind that particle is the Whole Truth, which does not give power to a problem, as unalert minds do. Open yourself to the vastness of the Whole Truth. Start by refusing to listen to the noise of a problem, for this enables you to hear an instructive message originating in a silent place above the problem.

THE SURE CURE FOR ALL PROBLEMS

Have you ever noticed how people always offer the same old cures for human problems? One group proposes new laws, a second preaches more love for one another, a third group confidently claims that a broader education will solve everything. And have you also noticed that nothing really changes? If an individual could see just that much —that nothing really changes, including himself—the shock could switch his mind from mechanical repetition to creative consciousness.

The next time you find yourself in a perplexing situation, do something entirely different. First of all, notice how your mind seeks anxiously for an answer, for relief, for reassurance. Now, break this pattern. Simply remain silent. Say to yourself, "What if I do not need the kind of answer I assume I do?" Stick with that. Do nothing else. Observe the inner result of this. Finally, realize that inner silence is always the perfect answer to all questions about life.

When a problem-hounded man complains, "I just don't know what to do," he often does not mean it. Deep inside he has a reservation which insists, "I know what to do, but people won't let me carry out my wonderful solutions." His false solutions always revolve around self-interest, but since this is unacceptable to his self-images of being humble, he pretends that he does not know what to do. When a man really does not know what to do, when he really accepts the unknown, he begins to know what to do.

The attempt to escape a problem is the problem. See the logic of this. When a man tries to escape, when he moves away from the problem, he divides himself into one man with a problem and another man who will escape the problem. In reality, there is no such division, so the escape must always fail, as the man sadly experiences. But when seeing that he is the problem itself, that he and his problem are one, he stops trying to escape because he sees there is no other course. In this state of intelligent acknowledgement of reality, he will not have the problem.

Gary C. commented, "You say that memory is rightly used for everyday tasks, such as cooking or typing, but memory must never be employed to solve inner problems. Why?" Answer: "Because you can't make fire by stirring ashes. Every moment of life is completely new, so when you permit memorized action to leap into the space reserved for present consciousness, creativity is blocked by mechanicalness. When your next problem arises, let your mind remain quiet before it, and watch what happens."

Have no fear in not knowing what to do about a problem. Fear activates its negative relatives of impulsiveness, ego-protection, and an anxious craving for security. Instead, let the mind be still. Never think of fighting, for an answer won by fighting will soon require another answer and another fight. The problem exists because of an agitated mind, so when the mind rests from its own agitation, there is no problem at all.

Remind yourself frequently of your purposes in reading this book. Write *My Purposes* across the top of a sheet of paper. List your aims by numbers, like this: 1. To take charge of my own life. 2. To end the endless circle of personal problems. 3. To discover what is truly valuable to me. 4. To enter the fascinating invisible world where everything is different.

HOW TO BE FREE FROM HARM

Suppose you want to know what Norway is like, so you ask several people who have lived there. One man tells you about its coastline, another about its high plateaus, while a third informant discusses the Norwegian people. While this is helpful, you want to know more, so you travel to Norway. Now you see Norway for yourself, you see how everything connects to form one complete country. This illustrates inner work. While you can be helped by others, you must yearn to see for yourself. Whatever you see for yourself becomes yours.

Connect a thought in this book with a specific problem. Let the thought erase the problem. The thought that suffering must not be a secret source of false excitement can end suffering. The thought that most people are frightened and confused can end the error of asking help from those who are in need of help themselves. The thought that there is something in a man which is stronger than his weakness can end discouragement.

Hugh C. asked, "What causes frustration?" Reply: "It is very simple. Frustration occurs when demands meet opposition. You want appreciation or excitement or comfort, which are denied, which turns your desire back against you, causing conflict. It is a false sense of self which creates these desires, for it frantically believes that its existence dedepends upon their fulfillment. When we see all this everything falls away—the false self, its demands, and our frustrations."

A person's psychological future can be predicted exactly. If he remains on the mechanical level of life, the prediction is for more unpleasant involvements, for a mechanical cause must produce a mechanical effect. If he rises to a conscious way of life, the prediction is for decreasing troubles and increaing self-composure, for the conscious man does not produce harmful causes and effects.

The following facts show you how to live untouched by human chaos. A negative event, such as public violence,

82

spreads out in a circle, just as an earthquake radiates its shock. An earthquake is mechanical, so everything else on its mechanical level vibrates to it, resulting in collapsed buildings and smashed cars. But an earthquake cannot harm the air, for air resides above the earthquake's level. See the tremendous significance? If you reside on the conscious level, you cannot be harmed by anything on mankind's mechanical level.

Realization is a dynamic force for self-transformation. Suppose a man finally realizes the solid fact that his level of psychic maturity makes his life whatever it is. And suppose that his life up to now has consisted of one frantic race after another, in a tiring attempt to find satisfaction, but which always ends in frustration. His realization would cause an explosion of consciousness, making him eager to raise his level of psychic maturity.

The reason a man fails to rise above his problems is because the wheel of an airplane cannot fly all by itself, and neither can a single wing or just the engine. Man attempts to fly by using just one part of himself at a time, one day by a borrowed opinion about life, and the next day by false elation. Only a whole airplane can fly, and only a self-unified human being can rise above human problems. He takes off as he ceases to be a problem to himself.

TAKE THE DIRECT ROUTE TO SELF-NEWNESS

Many years ago the engineers of a European monarch showed him a map of the route for a new railroad. The track curved back and forth in order to connect with various cities along the way. Taking a ruler, the monarch drew a straight line on the map, instructing, "Build it like that." Let that remind us to take the direct route to reality, and not make detours to old ideas simply because they seem familiar and reassuring.

A secretary asked, "What prevents people from seeing how practical it is to live by these principles? Why can't people see how superbly they work?" Answer: "The barrier is their refusal to see what *cannot* work. Ten thousand laws and ten thousand sermons cannot add one ounce of conscience to the mind, yet people continue to behave as if they can. An individual must become overwhelmingly weary of being impractical, for that invites the practical.''

If you have ever tried to convey an important message to a child over the telphone, you will understand why patience is a teacher's necessary virtue. The child's mind wanders, he asks irrelevant questions, he complains that he wants to run out and play. Over and over the teacher hears the lament, ''It's a terrible life.'' Over and over the teacher quietly tries to explain, ''Yes, but it need not remain that way.''

The sooner a student stops playing little games with his teacher the sooner an effective relationship can be established. The unaware student thinks that his petty pretensions and evasions are all quite clever and original, but the patient teacher sighs at what he has heard a thousand times before. Once a student abandons the game and admits his anxiety, the teacher can tell him, ''Don't try to be unafraid. Be just as scared as you are, but step forward. Every step taken while being afraid is a step away from fear.''

We should be encouraged, not discouraged, by seeing how much work we have to do on ourselves. It means we are awakening to our actual condition, we are seeing our self-defeating attitudes. People who live in self-images of being positive and wise and pleasant see no need whatever to work on themselves, so they remain in the suffering caused by living in dreamland. The worse we see ourselves to be, the more encouraged we should be, for if you know all about darkness, you also know about dawn.

A wise student is both gentle and firm with himself at the same time. While insisting upon diligent study, he is never harsh with himself. He has the quiet wisdom to see that he does not presently see. A student who finds himself acting unkindly can say to himself, ''I truly regret my present behavior, but I act like this because I am still a frightned and confused human being.'' With this attitude, he will not remain frightened and confused.

"We are forming a study group in Oregon," stated Jeffrey S., "and would appreciate suggestions for removing self-deception. We want to avoid time-consuming mistakes." Reply: "One valuable rule is to never bluff while discussing things. Let each person watch for this in himself and reject it. For instance, a man might state that he is now free from anger, when in fact he is simply hiding his anger from himself. This rule produces honest talk, which is a firm foundation for more honest and worthwhile talk."

THE RIGHT KIND OF SELF-TRUST

An airplane mechanic sees the connection between a stalled airplane and a broken wing, but man fails to connect his experiences with his inner condition. The inner and the outer are always equal in quality, in spite of appearances to the contrary. Evidence: We get along with others to the same degree we get along with ourselves. When not knowing what to do with troublesome experiences, we need only remove our attention from the outer scene to see what we can do with the mind,

Said a psychologist, "We are told to trust ourselves, but are also told to go beyond ourselves, which I don't undesrtand." Reply: "It depends upon what you mean by your *self*. If you take yourself as consisting of your unconscious self-labels, and then trust that false self, disaster results. If hard work has revealed you to be part of the Cosmic Whole, and you trust your insight, all is well."

Whenever you have a problem, look deeply into it. Somewhere down there is a basic problem, which when solved, clears away a dozen problems. The main problem is not a faulty marriage, but a faulty understanding of life itself. The main difficulty is not failure to win what we want from others, but failure to grasp the meaning of authentic success. Proof of this is plain. A wrongly-handled problem always returns, though in a new form. But when you thoroughly smash a stained dish, it never again takes shape.

Perhaps you have noticed how often the great teachers tell man that he has false ideas about himself. Man lives in dozens of imaginary self-pictures which he wrongly takes as his actual identity. But because a man never observes himself to see that it is so, he never believes anyone who tells him about it. I would like to end this paragraph with a single thought for your reflection: If you are not the person you think you are, you do not have the problems you think you have.

"I want to explore myself," said an inquirer, "but I am afraid of the strange creatures I may meet along the journey." Reply: "It is absolutely impossible for a fact about yourself to cause fear. No matter how terrible the fact may be, it is powerless in itself to either frighten or harm you. Fear is caused by your resistance to the fact, by misunderstanding it. Start your journey at once. Nothing but good can come from it."

The last thing on earth which should bother you is the sudden failure of your carefully laid plans. Do not take your plans as being *you* and the disruption of any plan will be as nothing to you. Your plans are not you; they only appear to be so because of that human mistake called *identification*. Identification means to wrongly assume that plans or possessions make up what we call the "self." Think this through to the very end, for it will free you from anxiety over unexpected changes in your daily affairs.

HOW TO RISE ABOVE YOURSELF

"Nothing fits into place. I am like a waitress who constantly serves the wrong dishes to diners, forcing me to start all over." This was how Sylvia K. described her problem. It is a good example of how a misunderstanding of our true nature drives us into impossible and frustrating tasks. Sylvia is still trying to force her personal ideas onto life, not seeing that oneness with life makes forcing unnecessary. She was assured, "You of yourself do not have to make life fit in place; it is already in place, and awareness of this sets you in your right place."

We do in fact maintain our own problems by opposing them. If loneliness was not opposed, it could not exist. If we stopped fighting anxiety toward the future, we would have no such anxiety. "Resist not evil." Why do we resist, oppose, and so support our own problems? Because opposition arouses a stimulation which we assume is an exciting life, but which is really desperation disguised as life. Cease to oppose your own problems and watch what happens.

It should be of no concern at all if you cannot as yet connect these principles with your present problems, whatever they may be. You may not see it as yet, but the connection is just as certain as the underground water pipe from your home to the water supply. The main point to remember is that solutions cannot be found by the conditioned mind; only consciousness sees rightness. For example, a man thinks he worries over money, when in fact he worries over being labeled a loser in society's money-game. When he banishes his false beliefs in labels, the problem vanishes.

Here is a major teaching of this chapter: It is just as pointless to try to solve an isolated problem as it is to try to beat back a single ocean wave. We must get out of the ocean altogether. Perhaps a man's problem is over-spending which keeps him in uncomfortable debt. Paying off one debt will not remove the cause of his compulsion, which is an attempt to feel secure by acquiring new objects. If he would only see how his insecurity persists in spite of his spending, he could catch a first glimpse of another way—the way of self-freedom.

When meeting a difficulty of any kind you must ask yourself, "Am I going to fight this difficulty or am I going to rise above it?" If you decide to fight you will have to fight endlessly and wearily, for it is the very battling with a problem which keeps it going. But if you decide to transcend it through insight, the problem disappears forever. It vanishes because you now see there was no individual *and* his problem, there was only an individual who *was* his problem. Rise above yourself.

Abandoned caves along the Jordan River tell an interesting story about life in ancient days. The caves exist at various heights on the riverbank, the lower ones almost touching the river, while others are near the top of the bank. At certain seasons, the river rose higher, forcing the occupants of the lower caves to climb to higher caves. When the river overflowed its banks completely, people were forced to abandon their caves altogether, to seek higher ground. That is exactly what suffering tries to do—to urge us to higher spiritual ground.

THE MOST INTELLIGENT TASK ON EARTH

Emmett J. requested, "Please connect these ideas with ill health." Reply: "When you see ill health in the light of these principles you see it quite differently; it is not a problem to you. For example, some people feel guilty over ill health because it exposes their illusion of having an all-powerful ego. Make your mind a lamp whose light illuminates everything around it, including matters of health."

Who is the man who sees at last? It is the man who refuses to settle, conclude, decide, the man who refuses comfort and security, who bears uncertainty to the bursting point and lets it burst. The bursting of the accumulated and the familiar permits entrance of something entirely different from the nervous knowing of society. With this bursting, a man becomes innocent again.

Whenever troubled about something, ask yourself, "Exactly *who* is troubled?" Now, if this troubled person does not truly represent your real nature, could the trouble exist except in wrong thinking? No, it could not. Do not pass by this idea. Stick with it for all you are worth, for it is the secret of secrets. Our false identifications cause all our troubles, but whatever has been wrongly constructed can also be destroyed. Other paragraphs in this book will bring this idea into clearer view.

The understanding of fear cures fear. Consciousness of the need for a wisdom beyond the self draws that wisdom to us. Insight into human affairs frees us from their conflict. Knowledge about false desires prevents them from pulling us into disaster. Awareness of the better way makes it a personal possession. Now having read this, ask yourself, "Is there a more intelligent task on earth than to win higher knowledge about myself and the world I inhabit?"

A boy found that his electric train would not work. His father wanted to convey a lesson in life as well as solve the immediate problem, so he told his son, "Always look for the most obvious cause." The boy discovered that the electric cord was unconnected to the wall socket. When our lives do not work as we wish, we must look for the most obvious cause. We will always find it to be our lack of connection with that part of the cosmic universe which dwells within our own psychic system.

REMEMBER THESE NOTABLE PRINCIPLES

1. Our single greatest problem is personal unawareness.
2. Check every offered solution for its authenticity.
3. As we solve ourselves we solve our problems.
4. Never permit the noise of a problem to overcome you.
5. Inner silence invites true and permanent solutions.
6. Connect these curing principles with a specific problem.
7. Feelings of frustration can be ended forever.
8. Any problem will start to crumble when honestly faced.
9. Do not fight difficulties, instead, understand them.
10. Problems are solved by rising above their level.

Chapter 7

HOW TO LIVE THE EASY AND NATURAL WAY

A kite soars in the sky when placed into a natural relationship with the wind. Efforts to make it fly without this relationship are futile and frustrating. The simplest of reasoning reveals the necessary alliance of kite and wind. But earthly-minded man, who rarely looks for anything above his own head, complains about his inability to ascend. The ascending man is one who has made an alliance with the higher processes of his own nature.

Life is controlled by being one with it. All other ideas about either self-control or social control are illusions which produce endless conflict. There is no controller and an object to be controlled, for we are not separate from the whole movement of life. As we realize our oneness with ourselves, all vain attempts to take control cease—and that is total control.

"How," asked Merle Y., "can we realize our oneness with life?" Response: "You realize it very clearly whenever the false self is absent. You don't feel separated from your son when he gets a larger piece of cake than you do, and you don't feel hurt or persecuted. Why? Because you are one with him; there is no sense of competition. But you may feel hurt when your neighbor draws a larger paycheck than you, which indicates a false sense of separation. Withdraw the false self from everything, and oneness is just there, naturally."

Is there a more appealing word in the language than *nat-*

ural? We are magically drawn toward the natural, whether it is a clear lake or a colorful bird or a moment of total sincerity between two people. We are attracted because we know without being told that the natural is the right. Everything in this book is intended to make the natural so attractive that all else fades out.

The difference between artificiality and naturalness can be illustrated by an actor during a performance. With memorized lines and practiced gestures, he must work hard to convince the audience that he is what he really is not. To be true to the role he must be false to himself. But with the departure of the audience, he has an entirely different relationship with his surroundings. He says what he actually feels, sits or stands as he likes. There is no longer a contradiction between his real self and his invented self, therefore, there is unconcern and casualness.

Inner truth flows outward with ease and naturalness. We need no preparations nor notes. Lao-tse, the Eastern mystic, was leaving China when frontier officials demanded the usual tax upon his possessions. Lao-tse said he possessed nothing but his philosophy, so the officials demanded that he write it down and leave it with them. Sitting down at the border, Lao-tse composed in three days one of the most fascinating of all books of esoteric teachings, the *Tao Teh King.*

NATURALNESS DELIVERS RELEASE AND RELIEF

Set an authentic toy boat into a pond and it floats. Set an ornamental boat made of metal into the pond and it sinks. The floating or sinking is conclusive evidence of their reality or artificiality. But most people are not as practical when testing the authenticity of their personal philosophies. They sink a dozen times a day, yet refuse the results of the test. The student of higher truth is wiser. By accepting the results of his daily tests, he learns the difference between reality and artificiality, which keeps him afloat.

Someone in class requested, ''Please show us an area

where we may be going wrong, then provide correction."
Reply: "Just about the most useless desire we can have is
the desire to impress other people. This is a dominating desire by which society lives—and gets hurt. There is a point
of intelligence in each one of you which wants nothing to
do with such misery. Release this intelligence, let it break
out, and watch how it makes you new."

When you first stand up for what is right—because it is
right, not for public applause—you feel a small disturbance.
It is similar to the slight apprehension felt when removing
a bandage from a healed wound. This feeling and increased self-health always go together, so have no concern
over it. You then rise above this feeling to a new emotion,
one of immense release and relief. This happens because
you are now one step higher in the pure air of cosmic truth.
Now sensing the healing power of rightness, you permit its
swift cure.

Our aim is to recognize rightness when we see it. That
is why daily watchfulness is so valuable. A brief meeting with a man may not enable us to recognize him a
week later, but by frequent contact with him we soon
know all his characteristics. Frequent contact with the
truth makes us certain, for it begins to match something already existing within us. A man in this state is unshakeable, independent, not a follower of another, but a self-
leader.

Lee G., whose interest in higher thought increased year-
ly, came to ask, "Why do so many people fail to see the
rewards of simple and decent behavior? What blocks awareness of self-benefit?" It was explained to Lee, "A hawk
never notices flowers; he sees only what he can pounce upon. This is why teachers emphasize the need for a new
kind of mental sight. This alone changes a man's nature."

Instead of trying to do something, try to understand something.
There is the entire secret for psychic rebirth. It cannot be
stated in a simpler or more practical way. We must remember it a dozen times a day. This truth serves as a guiding
light which ends useless and tiring attempts at self-rescue.

The same light reveals the nature of true action. Understanding itself is true action. If you are cold, and understand the healing power of warm sunlight, it is easy and natural to place yourself under it.

Any time you want an answer about anything at all, close your ears to the babble in the streets, remain apart from it, and remain quietly with your own unknowing. Just quietly realize that you do not know the answer; do nothing more than this. Will you do this much? Will you try it many times over the coming months? You can practice wherever you are, whether in the kitchen or factory or field. This may sound like a mystery, but it is right action.

HOW FALSE RESPONSIBILITIES FADE AWAY

Self-renewal is natural to the mind, so our task is to open ourselves to its freely flowing naturalness. It is like purifying the air in a room by opening opposing windows to a current of fresh air. We open fresh currents of thought by releasing yesterday's thoughts, especially those which seem to provide security, but which actually make life stale. Self-release brings self-renewal.

Nothing blocks inner progress more than the assumption that we must be what is called "intellectual" or "spiritual" or "authoratative." These are mere labels, like a book with an attractive title, but containing blank pages. We need only be sensible. We know what it means to be sensible. It means to cease to be our own punishment. It means to refuse to accept bitterness as a topic of our own mental conversations. The only salvation we need is our own sensibleness.

A small boy may stretch and strain in a vain effort to grasp an object above his head. His observing mother has no worry over his present inability, for she knows he can and will grow up to the height he wishes to reach. Spiritual growth proceeds without strain when we are truly humble. Many people want to govern others before maturing into self-government. They want to feel happiness before growing out of self-concern. We can reach the heights all right, but we must put growth before grasping.

When seeking aid, you don't need dramatic descriptions of the teacher you seek. Don't think you must locate an inspired mystic or a man blessed by cosmic power. He may be inspired or blessed, but searching with such labels in mind may lead you to someone who requires these labels in order to feel important. What you need is a man with a clear mind, a sane mind, a mind which sees you as someone to help, not as someone to cunningly exploit.

The man who neglects his present task of self-awareness skips a page in the instructive book, and when caught in a crisis he complains he cannot understand why this should have happened to him. Anthony K. testified, "I now see how much we pay for assistance and comfort from others who are just as lost as we are. This helps me to detach myself from false sources of help. If we absentmindedly walk into the lion's jaws, we have no complaint if they snap on us."

An authentic teacher helps others much like a parent teaches a child to cross the street safely. The parent's principal aim is to show the child how to cross all by himself. This is why all the great teachers stress self-reliance, self-reasoning, self-responsibility. A false teacher cannot even think of urging others toward self-dependence, for he has never found it himself. If you want to know how to find gold, ask a man who has found gold.

It may seem paradoxical, but when we take full responsibility for our lives, all responsibility disappears. Men have the illusion of having a duty to make the world spin properly, which is precisely what makes it wobble. The world spins all by itself, with us as a connected part of its whole operation. By taking the responsibility to understand this, false effort, false guilt, and false responsibility change into wholeness.

A DESCRIPTION OF A NOBLE LIFE

Imagine several people looking into a store window. Because she is interested in travel, one woman notices a costume from Mexico. A salesman sees a new book on business management. Everyone sees what interests him, to the exclusion of all else. In the inward life, this habit hampers progress. To correct it, study unfamiliar ideas. ''Your internal state is your world.'' Study that statement. ''A problem is solved by seeing that there is no problem outside of yourself.'' Investigate that idea.

If we try to find the truth without an equal effort to find ourselves, we wander down the wrong trail. That is like trying to find an apple seed outside of an apple. It is what we see in ourselves which saves us; nothing else can do it. The seeing is the saving. If a man could endure for five minutes all the things he has hidden from himself for fifty years, he would redeem those fifty years in those five minutes.

''You say,'' stated Shirley L., ''that detection of the wrong way helps us see the right way. Please explain.'' Reply: ''Say you are ambitious to get something. You observe anxiety involved in your efforts. Now, is anxiety *ever* right? Of course not. Your thinking is already clearer. Perhaps you now see your ambition as worthless, or maybe you sense the folly of pleasing unpleasant people as a means of gaining your goal. Awareness of wrongness reveals rightness.''

We think outwardly when we should think inwardly. Take that highly prized product called the leisurely life. We connect leisureliness with a holiday or with a good dinner with a few friends, not seeing that leisure is an entirely personal item, a mental state. This is a practical principle to remember, for when the mind is leisurely, so is your personal world, regardless of exterior turmoil.

Your goal is not to change your appearance before others, but to change your inner nature before your own eyes. Most people polish their external appearance because they do not sense the existence of their inner kingdom. Society can only show a man how to make the junk in his yard look like works of art, while esotericism shows him how to haul away the junk once and for all.

Unnaturalness covers and blocks naturalness. Our naturalness reveals its vast originality as our conscious work removes whatever is unnatural. It is like an alert stroller along the beach who discovers colorful shells uncovered by the retreating tide. We cannot make an effort to be natural, any more than we can try to become human beings, for that is our very nature. But we can see unnaturalness with such clarity that the very seeing becomes the force which removes it.

Ralph Waldo Emerson described the noble life by describing his friend, Henry David Thoreau. Emerson said that Thoreau had "no taste for elegant trifles . . . he chose to be rich by making his wants few . . . he was a speaker and actor of the truth . . . no opposition or ridicule had any weight with him . . . his senses were acute, his frame well-knit and hardy, his hands strong and skilful in the use of tools . . . there was a wonderful fitness of body and mind . . . he had a strong common sense . . . he had always a new resource . . . he understood the matter in hand at a glance . . . it was a pleasure and a privilege to walk with him . . . Thoreau was sincerity itself."

THE IMPORTANCE OF INSIGHT INTO NATURAL LAWS

If two of your friends are on the other side of a thick wall, you may not be able to recognize them by their voices. The wall prevents clear hearing. If you wish to recognize them, the wall must not remain between you and them. This is what we are now doing. In order to recognize the voice of truth, we are removing our psychological wall. For example, by removing traditional but false beliefs, we are able to hear the pure messages of our original nature.

Valuable self-knowledge can be won by examining this principle: *Winning in life is an entirely different thing from what it is commonly believed to be.* This challenges fixed assumptions that winning means to score material or psychological victories over another, or to be a person of fame or authority. This enables us to next see that winning in its true sense is to win over our own negativities.

Roger E. said he had been attracted to the class because it taught a new definition of success. He explained, "I was once nervous over my chances of winning financial success, but since succeeding I am simply nervous in a new way. There has to be something else." Comment: ".Every mental contradiction can be reconciled, which comes as you study your mind. You are studying yourself in this class, so you are doing just fine, but increase your effort. The speed of a man in a rowboat depends upon how deeply he dips his oars."

You should be more or less indifferent as to how you earn your living. It has no importance. Just be sure to perform inner work while performing outer work. The idea that one kind of work is more honorable or valuable than another is a delusion created by prideful men. And it makes no difference how much money you make or don't make. Your rewards are of an entirely different nature.

Mechanical work supplies the visible rewards of food and other daily necessities. Mechanical work, whether that of a carpenter or a professor, is work done without an aim of self-awakening. Conscious work provides the invisible rewards of self-harmony and other spiritual necessities. Conscious work, whether that of a carpenter or a professor, is work performed while using it for inner dawning. You can do mechanical work without receiving payment, but you can never do conscious work without payment, though at times it may seem delayed. You can learn to do mechanical work consciously, and when succeeding, you have overcome the world.

Reality is like a very generous employer, but one who pays your wages at irregular and unexpected times. If we have done our work as best we can, we need have no concern over time and nature of payment. It may be an intensified feeling that we are on the right track at last, or it may be a fresh delight in being both your own teacher and student. Dwight R. testified, "While working at my office one morning I suddenly realized that I need not torment myself with my own anger."

The understanding of natural laws plays an important part in self-betterment. Whether you call them natural or spiritual or psychological laws, it is all the same. Here are two laws for self-liberty: 1. Be willing to hear what you don't want to hear. 2. We can understand only that which we have risen above.

HOW TO GAIN COMPLETE VICTORY

Suppose you are an expert mountain climber who is teaching the skills of mountaineering to a class. When one thoughtless student criticizes your instructions, you are not disturbed; you simply understand the misunderstanding of the unaware student. Disturbance would have indicated uncertainty about yourself, but your personal expertness provided natural composure. The higher life provides a similar poise by which you casually take care of yourself in all conditions.

A man of true knowledge will take part in an intelligent discussion, but he will never argue. Arguing is the familiar attempt to prove oneself right while sensing his wrongness, Also, arguing serves as a shield against hearing truths one does not want to hear. A teacher knows he has touched a psychological sore spot when a pupil tries to argue.

Bill Y. had been impressed with the advice, "See a crisis as being a wrong response to life." For a week he directed his mind toward the understaning of this idea. At a meeting, he came up with this excellent report: "An event is not a crisis. An event merely *reveals* the endlessly whirling crisis within me. I am my own crisis. I now see how I cause my own grief by responding to life with this crisis-burdened self. I also see how the truth sets us free."

Review these wisdoms from Taoism: 1. Return to your original nature. 2. Do not interfere with the natural flow of life. 3. The contented man is rich. 4. True accomplishment comes without agitated effort. 5. Be aware of and reject artificiality. 6. Intelligent inaction is the highest form of action. 7. The loss of falseness quietly makes way for the gain of rightness.

A rancher bought a large section of land divided by a fence which separated half of the livestock from the other half. Wishing them to blend naturally, he removed the fence. By removing our mental fences of fixed opinions we blend with ourselves. This results in a completely natural religion, enjoyable and effortless. In this natural religion you are both your own teacher and student, both the musician and the music.

A student said, "I know that words have limited ability to describe an inner state, but will you please say a few words about peace—authentic peace." Response: "Peace exists when you have nothing to prove, or stated differently, when you have no self to prove. Did you get upset today because of a need to prove yourself right in some way? What if you realized the nonexistence of this self, which is really nothing but a bundle of memorized experiences? Who would have to prove anything? That is authentic peace."

No one can win over the man who has no need to win over anyone. And there is no need to win over anyone. To not win is to win. Try it. After enduring and ignoring the complaint of the old nature which frantically insists it must win, you will win. This is a new kind of victory, in which you do not win over people and events, but in which you win over the false belief that you must win. That is complete victory.

THE PRACTICAL POWER OF HIGHER PRINCIPLES

Eric T., a real estate executive, wanted to know, "How can these ideas help us understand a practical matter like money?" Reply: "When you understand how man's artificial laws have replaced natural laws, you will know everything you need to know about money. This sweeps out all problems and pains connected with money, for instance, you will never again be envious of anyone who earns more money than you. By the way, the next time you envy anyone about anything, study his face when he is unaware of being watched, then see whether you still envy him."

A child looking at a half-moon might assume that the moon consists of only half of a ball, of only what he can presently see. The adult who sees beyond the visual illusion knows that the moon is always full and complete. This simple illustration includes profound counsel for those who desire personal wholeness: "Don't assume. Get the facts."

No one likes substitutes. No one perfers to think about a pleasurable ocean voyage when he can experience it personally. Yet with astounding meekness human beings substitute an exterior appearance of self-control for authentic inner control, choose noisy excitement in place of creative psychic energy, agree to the domineering authority of others, instead of living from their own command. Substitutes appear to be bargains, but nothing is more costly.

If asked, "What country do you live in?" you would reply, "United States" or "Canada" or whatever. But consider your reply to, "What psychological country do you inhabit?" The question is supremely significant, for it relates to our state of happiness. If our psychological nation is war-like, we must share its terrors; if peaceful, so are we. Everything depends upon our spiritual citizenship, and if we don't like where we are, we can emigrate to a new nation.

See action as total life-action, instead of as individual and separate action. This makes life very simple and easy. No longer will you be burdened with false ideas about your responsibilities toward others. In this free state we are truly responsible, for we no longer spread nothing under the disguise of something. See yourself as one with all of life, for the action arising from that insight is pure and delightful.

There is no way reality can be prevented from flowing the way it flows. It is our vain attempts to force it to flow in the service of our imaginary needs which sets us in painful conflict with ourselves and nature. You are not separate from the flowing reality; you are that flowing reality. See this and you will not see anything else which conflicts with it. You will be what you see.

YOU CAN LIVE IN NATURAL NEWNESS

Asked Dr. Richard D., "How can we free the mind from a negative thought which tries to invade and injure us?" Answer: "By letting it go the instant it appears. People cling to negative thoughts because they love their nervous vibrations, which is false life. Sacrifice exciting vibrations, such as those aroused by envy or loss, in favor of true life."

Never plan your public behavior, either consciously or unconsciously. That wastes energy. To contrive impressive behavior only splits you into an artificial self and a natural self, making strain and conflict inevitable. Dare to take no thought for tomorrow, then, after passing through temporary discomfort, you will be natural, spontaneous, completely at ease.

Your work works for you. It builds itself. Self-certainty and self-government become your easy and natural way of life. Perhaps a few weeks ago you could perform only one small task, maybe the reading of informative books. But now you can do many things at the same time, with just as much ease as before. In addition to reading, you can now refuse to accept irritation as necessary, you can feel the thrill of taking a new responsibility for yourself, you can give no thought to a person who formerly frightened you.

Your life is quite capable of living itself naturally and easily. It does not need strained attempts at control. It is the attempt at control which causes loss of control. Have you ever noticed your lack of command at the moment you try to command? When demanding something from another person, you lose command of yourself. You and your life are one and the same, so there is no you *and* a life to command. When you are one with yourself, you are also one with life, which is full control and complete relaxation.

When a stream approaches a series of rocks, it has no preconceived plans for passing them. It does not see the rocks as opponents or as threats to its own existence. The very fluid nature of water tells it how to rightly meet everything in its path. Let this natural wisdom also be in you. Meet everything with a free and flexible mind which is not tied to past experiences. You will then meet all events without alarm, with quiet progress.

THE EASY AND NATURAL WAY IN REVIEW

1. A right relationship with life makes an easy life.
2. Our life is real when we are real.
3. Naturalness provides unshakeable self-independence.
4. Let self-knowledge abolish false responsibilities.
5. Self-unity dissolves all personal conflicts and pains.
6. Be assured that self-work always produces self-riches.
7. Study the natural laws explained in this book.
8. A right response is followed by a right feeling.
9. Do not accept substitutes for authentic life.
10. Live in a new way by living with these principles.

Chapter 8

THE ROYAL ROAD TO AUTHENTIC FREEDOM

I will show you how to become a unique human being. When people around you scream for what they want, don't join their screaming. If someone of the opposite sex offers to reduce your loneliness in exchange for what he or she wants from you, refuse the offer. While others praise self-reliance, you practice it. If a friend urges you to join him in aggression toward what he calls a common enemy, walk away. When authorities claim they can give you the answers to life, find your own answers by independent search.

At the end of a group session, Marcus K. asked, "May we have a helpful idea about authentic individuality to think about?" Reply: "Learn what it means to respond from *yourself* rather than from the words and acts of other people. Are others able to make you feel whatever you feel? Don't permit it. True individuality comes when you value your real nature more than you value the so-called security of having others around."

Everything depends upon what we take as normal, for whatever is classified as normal is never investigated and therefore never understood. The mind first accepts something as normal and then carelessly slides over to assume it is also necessary. Homes and offices are filled with weary people who take weariness as necessary. Don't share their belief. Remove yourself from their ranks. Freedom is normal.

Our freedom can be measured by the number of things we can walk away from. We cannot walk away from anything we falsely value, including exciting but pointless involvements. Non-attachment is the secret, and non-attachment is a product of valuing true life above all else. What a difference it would make if human beings loved their own lives, but instead they love their unconscious illusions, like children who hide forbidden and dangerous toys in the cellar. The spiritual adult knows how to walk casually. away from all that is not worth his attention.

A city-dweller heard of an ancient treasure which was supposed to have been buried by a fleeing monarch. Camping in the indicated valley, the man searched around. The longer he stayed the more he was fascinated by the surrounding beauty of the brooks and glens. Finally, losing all interest in the treasure, he determined to make a new life for himself in the lovely land. Similarly, our esoteric exploration changes our values, freeing us of an anxious search for rumored treasures.

Understanding comes to a self-working person something like this: The first ten times he does something wrong, he simply suffers from it. The next ten times he still suffers, but begins to notice his pain. The next ten times he knows he is doing wrong, but sees no other way. The next ten times it dawns on him that his abandonment of the wrong way, without knowing the right way in advance, is the only right procedure. At this point, the wrong falls away to make room for the right. This procedure can correct anything wrong in anyone's life.

DECLARE YOUR OWN LIBERTY

Marjorie D. opened the dialogue by describing her condition. "I feel," she explained, "like I am living under a pain-killing drug that will wear off any minute. I don't want soothing counsel any more; I want practical help." With this right attitude, Marjorie began her studies of higher thought. It resulted in what she really wanted—a sensing of a freedom she had never felt before.

Imagine yourself watching some children playing a game about kings and castles. One crying child appeals to you, "Make him give me my crown!" Another upset child asks you, "How can I own my own castle?" You patiently explain that their requests and questions are based on imaginary activities, therefore, there is really no reply. Similarly, a teacher tells mankind, "I don't want you to cry anymore, so listen to what I say. Your strivings are false because your values are false. Awaken! See the game you are playing! Let reality replace imagination, and then you will not cry anymore."

A man gives considerable thought to being right with his family or his employer or his club, but completely overlooks the need to be right with himself. This happens because he fails to see his oneness with all of life. Having divided himself by the labels of "family man" and "club member," he is at the mercy of his divisions, for the family or club may dissolve. His task is to pull himself together, to be right with himself. His awareness of self-division is his start toward self-unity.

Dare to go beyond your present mind! A wall erected around the mind prevents a man's thoughts from going beyond that wall. All the freshness and originality beyond the mental wall cannot be seen nor experienced. Because a man cannot glimpse the carefree way of life, he will scorn the very idea of its existence. It is this rejection of the unknown which erects the self-imprisoning wall. But by daring to challenge his monotonous life behind the wall, a man catches his first glimpse of the freshness beyond it.

A man begins to be on his own in the world when he first sees it is not frightening or lonely to stand by himself, as he formerly assumed. That insight also reveals he was frightened and lonely precisely because he was *not* on his own. Having found himself, he sees how right the classic teachers were by proclaiming the presence of the kingdom of heaven within.

When you think of the word *liberty* you should never let your mind leap to an association with certain other words, like *political, economic, social, religious.* True liberty does not associate with these words; it only appears so. Liberty connects with only one area, which can be described by the words *inner, mental, individual.*

Man's life on earth is what it is because he spends almost every moment of his life trying to cover up his anxieties instead of understanding and dissolving them. It is this inner frenzy which produces every earthly problem. You must declare, "I am no longer going to be a part of this frenzy," and you must say it without any regard for the consequences to you. You will find that the final consequences can be nothing but good.

APPLY THESE METHODS FOR SELF-FREEDOM

In order to be free, we must clearly see how unfree we are, which is a task calling for all the best in us. It is extremely difficult to get past a man's imagination of himself as being a perfectly free individual. The healthy task appointed to Richard E. was to notice how unfree he was of daily irritations. The work of Lila A. was to see how easily her opinions were swayed by various authorities. Only the man who realizes his imprisonment will have the power to escape.

Complaints against life for denying our desires are unjustified. Both the complaint and its pain will evaporate if we make an effort to understand one characteristic of desire. Desire always splits itself into Yes and No, that is, by desiring something we must expect an answer of either Yes or No. A man desires riches or fame or popularity because he wrongly thinks they can relieve his underground insecurity. By seeing through this false reaching for security, the desire fades, followed by the fading of Yes and No, followed by the ending of complaint and anxiety.

Paul S. spoke up in class, "I am enthralled by your statement that we need not plead for anything. Will you please go over it again?" Response: "You don't have to plead for love or money or security or anything else. Stop pleading, just to see what happens. Stick with whatever happens; don't be afraid of it. Then you will know why it is completely unnecessary to plead with anyone for anything. You qualify for this by first seeing, with great honesty, that you *are* pleading, but are covering it up with fancy labels."

Literary classics such as Dante's *Divine Comedy* and Bunyan's *Pilgrim's Progress* successfully illustrate one phase of our inner journey toward the light. The path naturally passes through what is called "hell" or perhaps "the valley of humiliation." This experience is simply the shock we feel when finally facing our wild and suppressed inner nature. Our courage in taking the shocks proves we are the master of these dreadful dragons after all. We then proceed to "paradise," which is a state of freedom and consciousness.

Men live under their self-created system in which psychological advantage and disadvantage alternate with each other. The doctor has advantage over his patient, such as in fees, but is at a disadvantage with his lawyer. A free man, a man who understands life, does not seek advantage, therefore, he is free of disadvantage, for the two always go together. A free man has the usual human relationships, and though it may appear to others that he is sometimes at a disadvantage, he knows better. Being psychologically free, he handles everything, including financial matters, without seeing them as problems.

Imagine yourself seated by a window with a telescope. Looking out through it, you see only a blur of hills and meadows. Knowing it is not a true scene, you adjust the telescope until it functions correctly. Inwardly, every person senses that he is not getting a true scene of life, but he does not know how to correct his vision. Your application of these principles will provide true vision.

HOW TO LIVE FROM YOUR OWN MIND

Man takes his imaginary life for real life, while mistaking real life for imaginary life. He rarely questions the difference, even when the difference bruises him. Because of this, all of society's actions for human betterment are false. It is like knocking a man down with one hand and helping him up with the other, while calling the help a heroic act. The progress we have made in science and agriculture came not *because* of human nature, but in *spite* of it.

Treasure your independence above all. Don't trade your mental liberty for trinkets from men. Lonely and frightened people try to reduce their anxiety by pleasing other people in order to gain their friendship. Refuse to do this. At first, your anxiety may seem to increase, but stick with your refusal, pass through it, and fear fades like fog in sunlight. William Blake, the English mystic, declined the offer to teach the king's children, seeing in it the loss of his freedom and privacy.

To make your own rules in life does not mean to publicly rebel against man-made rules. That is a waste of energy which accomplishes nothing. The fierce wind which topples the tree is on the same level as the tree. To live by your own rules means you have first discovered the rules of your original nature. In this discovery resides a new kind of power— the power of innocence.

To think for yourself means to not think from your habitual self. What a man calls his self is simply a hardened collection of personal habits and desires and judgments. He can only harm himself by thinking with this collected self, for it is inevitably opposed by millions of other collected selves in the world. He can think for himself by refusing his collected self, to think with his Cosmic Mind, in which there is no opposition.

No values have value unless they come straight from your unshackled self. Don't listen to what others insist is valuable; they are all wrong and their anxious insistence proves it. When others solemnly inform you that you cannot have their prize unless you dance to their tune, don't dance. They will not know what to do with the refused prize, but you will know what to do. Walk out of their kind of life into your own life.

"I am aware of the many false values I must give up," said Charlotte B., "but I also know how tightly they grip us. I refer to false values like the compulsive need to appear to be in the right on any question." Response: "When a slave first escapes a cruel master he has no concern for the scanty possessions he must leave behind; freedom alone matters. Try to feel this idea intensely, after which everything connected with the old slave days will be nothing."

REMOVE OBSTACLES FROM YOUR PATH

Lester Y. asked, "You say we can cancel out past mistakes completely, but how can the memory of errors be suppressed?" Answer: "Attempts to suppress memory only causes unconscious conflict and neurosis. Cancelling comes by detaching your sense of self from the past error. When you live only in the present moment, not identifying yourself with the past mistake, its hold on you vanishes. In this new state you will not repeat the error, for now you understand."

Our inner health is served by seeing everything there is to see about a particular idea. The barrier to this is the unconscious assumption that we already see everything, when in fact we see only our side. It is like five people, each in a separate room, each having one-fifth of a map, which he takes as the whole scene. But if they come together, each has the whole. Take an idea and try to bring all its parts together. It creates a delightful wholeness.

We understand ourselves according to the number of facts we can see about ourselves all at once. Here is a man who sees his depression. He increases his understanding by seeing that depression is caused by wrong self-views. Next he sees that one of these wrong views is that others should appreciate him more. Next he realizes that requiring appreciation can only make him demanding and nervous. Continuing to add facts, he next realizes that his true nature is complete in itself, that it is free from demands and tensions. Anyone can work in this way to understand and free himself.

If a child's wagon stands between you and a doorway, you remove the wagon and pass through. Our work consists largely of removing whatever stands between us and our destinations. Mr. R. became aware of pride standing in the way of reason. Mrs. F. saw how mechanical reactions blocked right reactions. Miss H. realized that lack of knowledge stood between her and happiness. Find your obstacles and remove them.

A member of a Hawaiian study group stated, "The last thing we want is to appear ridiculous, but I can think of nothing more ridiculous than to remain a prisoner of our own folly. May we have a comment on this?" Reply: "Yes, man sits in his cell with anxious eyes, hoping for someone to come along with a key, never realizing he has it in his own pocket. Self-liberation is the act of searching ourselves for the key we think belongs to someone else."

You are free when someone close to you falls into public disgrace and you take it with pure understanding instead of self-concerned distress. You are free when you ignore all talk about organized religion because you know that an individual's inner state is his religion. You are free when you know the truth without needing to have others know that you know. You are free when you have the power to hurt another without getting hurt in return and you do not hurt him.

DOUBLE YOUR INTEREST IN THESE IDEAS

At a Sunday afternoon lecture, Lewis G. asked, "How can we listen more attentively to these ideas?" Reply: "People pay attention according to the depth of their interest. Let someone in this audience ask a question about sex and everyone else jumps awake. So the aim is to strengthen attention, which comes with the increasing insight that we actually inhabit a haunted house, not a fairyland palace.''

When your cozy little house comes crashing down upon your head, let it crash completely. Don't offer the slightest resistance or protest. Listen! What is happening is the very opposite of what you think is happening. All crashes are the crashes of haunted houses which give the illusion of coziness, for a house built on the foundation of consciousness cannot crash. Don't try to rebuild that familiar house; you will only return to the same unconscious nervousness. Instead, just let everything crash in any way it wishes, while you stand by without fear or despair. You will then see what it means to live in open space.

We must dare to cut ourselves off from attractive-but-negative influences. The influence could be a person or an activity or a personal thought. Sam D. sensed the hostility of a certain friend toward spiritual matters, so the friendship was dissolved. Inez L. recognized the false pleasure of imagining herself the center of attention, so the mental scene was rejected. Practice with this project makes it increasingly easier. No man plays with an attractive package when realizing that it contains a time bomb.

Through these truths you remain in charge of yourself at all times. Most people do not possess self-command because they live from adopted roles, instead of from themselves. Role-playing provides the appearance of self-command, but it is unreal, like an actor playing an army officer. People get nervous when a role is exposed, for example, a driver impatiently honks his horn at another driver, only to discover in embarrassment that the other man is his next-door neighbor. Authentic self-command is never embarrassed, for its inner trueness never permits exterior artificiality.

Command the whole of yourself and you command the parts. It is like a capable business executive who controls every department of his company. As an example, you will be in command of your facial expressions. You will be conscious of how your face appears to others, but there will be no uncomfortable masks. You will know when to smile and when not to smile, but there will be no contrived motives. When you are yourself, your face is itself also, which saves so much strain.

A free man possesses a unique indifference. He is not indifferent to human suffering, in fact, he alone expresses true compassion, for a trapped man can only feign compassion, with self-interest behind it. The free man's indifference is a part of his total freedom, for example, he has no flattering self-images which must be protected against slander and insult. Others do not know this, of course, for wolves howling at the moon have no idea of the moon's indifference. His unique indifference is part of his peace.

SECRETS FOR AUTHENTIC INDEPENDENCE

Man is forever dissatisfied with his satisfactions. Give a horse oats and shelter and you can train him to no longer rebel against the saddle on his back, but that saddle still remains an unnatural burden. The entire social system is dedicated to the glorification of conformity, which is called freedom. You are never obligated to accept anything which is unnatural to *you*. You do not have to accept your own unhappiness.

Imagine a dozen cooks gathered around a huge kettle of untasty soup. Each tastes the soup and then adds an ingredient which he insists will improve its flavor, but it only gets worse. Finally, one cook with a clearer taste than the others, refuses to participate in the foolishness any longer. He sets about to make his own soup, which turns out just right. When an individual finally realizes that society cannot be changed by adding more of the same wrong ingredients, he refuses to participate in the deceptive game any longer.

Don't let other people set the price on your life. Set your own price, and set it so high that no one will be able to buy you with pretty bubbles which soon burst. And don't bargain with your life, for you will be paid in counterfeit money which will be painfully felt as counterfeit. Do this: Be *more* pained by the counterfeit until it reaches a severe intensity. For out of that intense dissatisfaction will arise your love for the real. Now you will no longer trade with others, for your solid gold has nothing in common with the counterfeit.

Would you like to know a great secret for complete independence from others? Here it is: You can never be punished or hurt by a self-defect which you see before another sees it. To be clearly conscious of fault in yourself completely disarms others, making them powerless to harm you. Additionally, this self-insight begins to rub away the defect itself.

A person who unconsciously behaves like a sheep will be treated like a sheep. If a man wants to know why he is treated the way he is, he can examine whether his psychic level is that of a sheep or of a lion. An ancient parable tells about a lion who was born in a sheepfold. Growing up with the sheep, he thought he was one of them. When a wolf crept near, the lion bleated fearfully and ran away. One day a kingly lion passed by and saw the strange sight of the young lion grazing among the sheep. The amazed lion called out, "What are you doing among sheep? You are a lion. Come out and live like a lion."

Dr. Robert M. asked, "You have said that immediate self-harmony is possible, but how can this be so when we are so far away from its Supreme Source?" Reply: "You are always in the Source. You are never outside it. It appears that you are outside because imagination has replaced awareness. Don't wander around in dreamland; come back to yourself and notice where you are. If a king in his palace has a nightmare of being in a burning desert, but awakens, where is he?"

HOW LIBERTY CAN DAWN FOR YOU

A pupil asked a master of Taoism, "To do what is right, we must know what is right—but how?" The master replied, "A small child might think a bar of soap is a piece of candy, but his own taste tells him something else. Your sense of wrongness is always right. If a thousand authorities tell you it is permissible to hurt another, a single voice in you says it is not. Listen to this voice."

You can hear answers from two sources. You can hear them from an individual who has liberated himself, and you can hear them from your own awakening nature. The advantage of answers from a free man is their purity; they are not mixed with error, as is the case with the student. However, since the student is with himself twenty-four hours a day, he can learn to listen carefully. In time, fact is clearly distinguished from fiction.

Edward L. asked, "How does freedom from self-danger free us from others who may be dangerous?" Reply: "A man under the illusion that others can fulfill him will resort to various trickeries to get what he wants from them. But with self-work comes awareness that tricking others is the same as self-slapping. Now feeling this painful slapping consciously for the first time, he sees what he is doing to himself, which ends his self-danger. Having seen through himself, he now sees through the trickery of others. He is no longer the gullible victim of those who offer him so-called love and assistance."

People choose the bad only because they mistakenly assume it is the good. Experience and suffering try to show us our mistake, which means we must listen to the lessons. A man who endures the boring or harmful company of others because he is lonely could begin to see the worthlessness of such company. Later, with self-freedom, human associations will never be a problem to him, for a bird that can fly at all can fly either with others or all alone.

There is legitimate comfort and there is illegitimate comfort along the spiritual path. It is illegitimate when we feel good because a friend says something nice about us just after an enemy has said something bad. True comfort comes after we have patiently endured humiliation of the ego to the point where something cracks. This cracking is the dawning of liberty.

A sparrow hopped along the ground until it was halted by a chain link fence. After several frustrating attempts to force its way through one of the openings, it paused long enough to glance upward—and instantly flew over the top. Similarly, human beings frustrate themselves by trying to force life to conform to their hardened ideas. To help them, the great teachers have repeated, "Stop fighting. There is another way. Look up!"

PEAKS OF TRUTH ABOUT SELF-FREEDOM

1. True individuality is available to all who want it.
2. Value self-freedom above all the lures of society.
3. Self-work arouses a refreshing sense of inner liberty.
4. Dare to adventure beyond your present mental borders.
5. Remember that liberty is inner, mental, individual.
6. Awareness of non-freedom is a first step toward freedom.
7. We need not plead with anyone for anything.
8. These truths have power to cancel the past completely.
9. Today, double your enthusiasm for these wealthy ideas.
10. Command yourself and you command all of life.

Chapter 9

HOW TO GAIN CONFIDENCE AND COMMAND

The reason why you should be confident can be summarized in three facts: 1. An entirely new world exists. 2. Sincere men and women throughout the ages have entered it. 3. You can also enter it. In this new world, your morning will be unique. You know your coming day will be all right because you also know there is nothing in you which will lose control. You feel and live within the conquering power, unlike those who are still victims of the disturbances in the world.

Take the attitude that the heights attained by others can also be attained by you. The purpose in this is to detach dependency upon successful people, which then activates your own powers. Obviously, this must not be done in a spirit of competition or in an attempt to be superior, for these wrong motives are weights on our wings. Just realize that the higher world is open to all who really want it, then go all the way.

Sometimes a seeker is discouraged by a fact which should rightly encourage him, as with Jeffrey G. Worried over his possible insincerity, Jeffrey was cheered by hearing, "It is pure imagination that anyone starts on the path with one hundred percent sincerity, or even fifty or ten percent. One percent is all a man possesses at the start, and even this wavers at first. But one percent is tremendous, for like a magnet, it attracts more sincerity."

A businessman would think himself in heaven if every

move he made turned into instant profit. I wonder how many people know there is a way to live in which everything turns into benefit? People who have this realization, even dimly at first, make swift progress. When all feels lost, they remind themselves that this is an inner feeling, but not a spiritual fact. If faced with a difficult decision, they know that their true nature is not permanently endangered, regardless of their decision.

Suppose a chemistry student is assigned the task of making a certain kind of perfume. Taking a book of formulas, he works at it, but everything goes wrong. Checking it out, he discovers he had selected the wrong formula. Locating the right formula, he produces the perfume. In our life-task, we need not be dismayed if everything goes wrong. We need only realize that we have somehow selected the wrong formula. That realization in itself is a guide to the right one.

There is an intelligence in you which is superior to everything which is faulty in both you and in the rest of the world. You become aware of its existence by wanting the awareness. This means you must never close your eyes to any event which you or another thinks is disastrous. Just let your natural intelligence go to work on this seemingly distressful situation, and watch the result. You prove you are smarter than the fox by catching the fox.

ENCOURAGING FACTS ABOUT SELF-CONFIDENCE

People sometimes react to a presented truth, "But that does not solve my personal problem. It discusses self-insight, but my specific problem is chronic worry over money." This is a failure to see that all problems have the same source—an unenlightened mind. This is an encouraging fact to see, for it means that self-enlightenment cures everything. The truth which ends depression also ends family quarrels. Freedom from self-defeating thoughts is also freedom from actions which are later regretted.

"I find myself doing exactly what you cautioned us against," said Lowell O. "I resist the inflow of original ideas. It is remarkable how I can see my nervous defenses against even small threats to my old ways. How can I stop fearing the shattering of my habitual life?" Reply: "Remember that the shattering you fear is only the shattering of another mental wall which has kept you separated from yourself. This will encourage you."

From the esoteric viewpoint, courage is to freely admit that one is unhappy, confused, and without authentic strength or knowledge or purpose. Such courage is the same as humility. Out of this courage arises receptivity to higher truths, which results in newness of being. It is one of the strangely cheerful facts of life that a man's own neurosis, wisely used, can drive him all the way to salvation.

An authentic spiritual doctor gives his patient something almost unobtainable elsewhere, namely, total permission to be as lost as he really is. Not only can the patient now sit back and "be himself," but he can dimly glimpse what has been driving him nearly mad over the years. He senses that he does not consist of two opposite selves, with one able to operate upon and reform the other, but that he is in fact a single, self-complete individual. This is both surprising and delightful, for it proves that he had nothing to do all along except to understand his true nature. This produces true change.

Never hesitate to expose self-weakness to yourself. It is not disgraceful to see weakness, it is the beginning of strength and wisdom. Take a man who is cheated by someone. The chief reason he feels resentful is because his gullibility is exposed. But a willingness to learn from the humiliation will remove his gullibility. We must remember that the truth which saddens our ego is the very same truth which cheers our spirit.

Everything about higher thought is good news. No matter how new or different or surprising it may be, it is always good news. Keep this in mind, especially during those times when a truth clashes with a belief you know you must abandon but are reluctant to do so. What wise man prefers a pebble when he can exchange it for a diamond?

An English merchant was exploring an old country house he had just inherited. Among the assorted items piled up in an unused room was a dusty scroll. Upon unrolling and spreading it out, the merchant saw an original painting by one of the great English artists of an earlier century. The discovery was made because someone had been interested enough in exploring and unrolling the unknown. Any time we become interested enough in discovering the riches of the mind, we can do so.

HOW TO WIN AUTHENTIC POWER

You have power over every person and circumstance which you do not fight. You are under the power of every person and circumstance which you fight. The harmful fighting is done by a false thought which insists it is separate from cosmic circumstances. So it is the very attempt to have power which makes us powerless. And it is the abandonment of all attempts to have power which blends us with cosmic power which conquers all.

True courage belongs to the person who voluntarily gives up his fondness for having enemies. An unawakened man clings desperately to his enemies, for without them he would feel empty, unimportant. He fears the loss of the agitation supplied by enemies, for he is deceived into thinking that agitation is an exciting way of life. Can we give up one enemy today, whether a person or stubborn machine or cloudy day? We can do that much in order to express the courage for conquest.

Lucy F. said, "Your teachings answer the questions I have asked for years, but the odds seem so dreadfully against my personal experiencing of the answers." Reply: "If the odds seem incredible against you, I want you to ignore the odds completely. They have only the pseudo-power you unknowingly give them. Now, let's work together to see this as a liberating fact."

Do not let anything you do not presently understand make you doubt anything you do understand. You know the value and necessity of thinking from your own mind. That is internally secure and can never be taken from you by confusion about a family problem. You feel the rightness of studying good books on higher thought. That good action is independent of any doubts you may have about your future. A pearl among pebbles remains a pearl. Never forget that.

Just as a rancher watches carefully to prevent marauding animals from carrying off his livestock, so must we watch to prevent loss of vital energies. What is carrying off your strength? Unconscious and unnecessary haste? What is draining your power for clear thought? Negative emotions? Let watchfulness prevent loss.

Friends of Henry David Thoreau used to send him rare plants discovered in their local fields. During his customary walks, Thoreau found the same plants growing in his own meadows. Our experience with a new reality comes in a similar manner. It comes to us first as a lecture or a word or an impression, and we are rightly pleased with the exterior source which delivered it. Then, our own exploration proves it was always a part of our world, but now we are able to recognize it.

Spiritual literature will appear entirely different to your deepening perception. For example, you will see something you never saw before in New Testament teachings such as: "The former things are passed away . . . . There is no fear in love . . . . Judge not according to the appearance . . . . The truth shall make you free . . . . When I became a man, I put away childish things . . . . Be vigilant . . . . Let all things be done decently . . . . No man can serve two masters . . . . Ask, and it shall be given you . . . . Study to be quiet . . . . The things which are not seen are eternal."

HOW TO RESPOND RIGHTLY TO LIFE

A class member requested, "Please show us how to

have more courage and daring toward inner exploration.''
The class heard, ''Dare to think about ideas you have never
dared to think about before. Take the idea that you are
not at all the kind of a person you imagine yourself to be.
Will you dare to think deeply and persistently about this?
Remember that man's chief illusion is his illusion that he is
not living in illusion about himself.''

What we must do is to withdraw the usual sense of self
out of what happens to us. Over the years we have acquired hundreds of reactions and feelings and attitudes
which make up what we call the ''self.'' It is this habitual
self which responds to life, sometimes with disappointment
and other times with a shaky elation. To respond rightly,
we must and can respond without reference to this fictitious self. The very understanding of this false self-structure
provides wisdom and strength for responding in a new and
refreshing way.

There is no greater act of authentic courage than to refuse to repeat today what was said yesterday with so much
apparent confidence and conviction. The refusal to take
pride and refuge in a memorized self-picture of a minute
or ten years ago signals a breakthrough toward the understanding of, ''I am as free as Nature first made man.''
(John Dryden) To live truly is to live within the purity of
each new moment, untouched by distorting memories about
ourselves.

A man who had to journey to another city felt himself
incapable of completing the trip, and said so to his friend
Plato. Being practical-minded, as are all true philosophers,
Plato provided the man with some solid logic. ''The steps
you take around your home in a single day,'' said Plato,
''would easily reach your destination if they were taken in
a straight line.'' And so do we have the necessary strength
to reach our psychic destinations. We need only expend it
in the right direction.

You should remember how easy it is to start moving in
the right direction. To see how self-justification prevents
self-transformation is a fine start. To really mean it when

you declare that you want out of the social trap is another fine start. Start every day with little ideas like these, and some day you will be highly happy that you did.

It is never a problem to not understand a new idea. A problem arises only when we react wrongly to the fresh information. Wrong reactions: 1. To feel humiliated because we do not grasp it. 2. To push it aside without thoughtful reflection. 3. To feel incapable of understanding it. Right reactions: 1. To be pleased at the new discovery. 2. To blend it with previously understood ideas. 3. To welcome it as another upward step.

People sadly sigh, "I wish I could believe in self-transformation, but I am too depressed to believe in anything." The answer is, we don't have to believe in anything; we need only experiment with self-change. One doubter was told, "Do you think the great teachers, men like Plotinus and Shankara would have provided their techniques unless men were capable of making them work? You can be your own proof of their workability."

YOU CAN BE STRONG RIGHT NOW

Probably the five most pleasing words a man or woman can ever hear are, "You are doing just fine!" Such encouragement has its place in our inner task, but has a special meaning, a meaning which would baffle those who dwell in deep psychic sleep. We are doing just fine when we see with increasing clarity just how great a problem we are to ourselves! The sleeping person refuses such insight, for it threatens his flattering self-pictures. But the awakening person senses that the seeing of the problem is the same as the ending of the problem, which proves that he is truly doing just fine!

You can be strong any time you wish. Time and circumstance and habit and feelings have no power to prevent you from being strong right now. You can even be strong when part of you does not wish to be strong. This is achieved by being strong where true strength originates—by sincerely desiring to be above any weakness which tries to possess you. Weakness has no authentic power over you at all.

Requested Eric C., "Please show us how to rise above feeling offended." Reply: "If a mechanical robot made a rude remark to you, you would not feel offended, for your ego would not feel threatened by a mere machine. But because you fail to see that most people are equally mechanical, you attribute an ego to them, which causes your ego to think they can harm you. When you deeply see the man-machine behind human personality, you cannot be offended."

The self-knowing man can do something which millions of other people can only yearn to do—*he can trust himself.* We can discover his happy secret by examining the inner nature of a self-divided man. It consists of dozens of "selves" which fight with each other in taking him over for a few minutes at a time. Living in a state of psychic riot, he is thrilled one minute and dejected the next. One part of him is a danger to another part. So what can be trusted? Nothing. The self-knowing man has cleared his mental streets of these rioters, leaving him with a whole and healthy mind, which can be trusted completely.

A careless thinker might believe he lives in self-trust, when in fact he lives in other-dependency. He depends upon his family or his career for feelings of security, but fearfully senses their possible loss. Self-trust depends upon nothing. It is a state of oneness, completeness, therefore, even the idea of having outside support has no meaning. In self-trust there is no *you* and *something else which is trusted;* there is only a single state of trust. You trust yourself because you are trust itself. This is a totally new state which comes with the insight that you are really one with yourself after all.

Think of someone you are fearfully depending upon. Say to this person, silently and without hostility, "Starting today, you have nothing of a psychological nature to give me—not love or security or comfort or anything else." You

don't have to fully understand what you are doing; just do
it. Continue with your daily life with this declaration in
mind. It will work quietly within you to abolish fearful dependency.

UNDERSTAND THIS GREAT COSMIC PROCESS

Each time you consent to a loss you make a gain.
Give hours of special study to this tremendous cosmic process. Lose the need to appear impressive and important
and we no longer bend under the burden of artificial behavior. Give up interpreting truthful ideas according to personal preferences and we gain accurate mental guidance.
Abandon compulsive duties based on self-pleasing self-
images and we no longer sacrifice our life to others.

Hermann Hesse, the noted author of esoteric novels,
realized the need to lose both his self-esteem and his self-
contempt. What does this mean? It means to no longer
divide the mind with opposite thoughts about oneself. The
mind occupied with self-esteem will constantly slip over to
the other side of self-contempt. Both positions are false.
There is a third way of thinking which is above these opposites. It comes when our invented selves evaporate in the
light of understanding.

One by one the lights come on. You will understand
what the teachers mean when they say a man lives in false
and ruinous self-images. It simply means he has come to
believe his own advertising. You will feel great release
from a false sense of responsibility toward others. This
comes as you realize you cannot help a man out of a pit
unless you yourself are out of it.

People remark, "I am aware of the many wrong parts
within me, but I hope there is at least one part which is
right!" There is one thing which the false parts within us
cannot do; it cannot have a sustained and earnest interest
in these ideas, for these ideas mean the end of their tyranny. Sincere interest is right; it can never be wrong. And
happily, rightness has a natural talent for doubling itself.

Ronald F., a school teacher, asked, "Why can't we understand many of the answers to the questions we ask about the higher life?'' He was told, ''Because a question cannot be answered on its own level. It is like standing in a valley and asking a man on the mountaintop to describe the weather up there. We are too far away to hear the answer, but if we climb, we hear.''

A Japanese emperor wished to reward his favorite prime minister, so he gave him a scroll of personal safety. The scroll gave the minister immunity from prosecution in the future. Hiding the scroll in the wall, the minister forgot about it. Many years later, an evil court official sought to confiscate the minister's property, but was thwarted when the dusty scroll was removed from the wall and unrolled. This illustrates why we should never be discouraged by feeling we are not learning anything. We are learning many things which will come at the right time and place to aid us.

SEEK THIS NEW KIND OF CONFIDENCE

People ask, ''But why can't I grasp these higher truths which would heal me?'' Answer: ''For the same reason we cannot have a dollar's worth of groceries for a dime. In order to have more, we must pay out with more valuable coins of consciousness. We earn more of the necessary mental money by applying ourselves to our lessons, like that of honest self-facing.''

You don't have to know where you are going. In fact, you must not know where you are going. If you know where you are going you are not going anywhere; it is just the tricky conditioned mind trying to feel secure by putting a new cloak over the old way and hailing it as the new. Down with what people call security, which is no security at all. Have you noticed that? You are not divided from life and never were; true knowing consists of realizing this. Abandon acquired knowing and there is universal knowing.

Nancy R. exclaimed in a perplexed voice, ''There are

so many new words to learn! I wonder whether I can ever understand the deeper meaning of words like self-awareness and self-unity.'' Response: ''When you first learn to play a piano, you learn words like octave and tone. But once you learn to play, you just play, leaving words out of it. It works like this in your inner life, so be cheerful!''

We are after an entirely new kind of confidence. It is a confidence which you do not have to think about. To think about confidence is lack of confidence, for then there is separation between the person wanting confidence and confidence itself. You do not think about water when your body is satisfied; you think about water only when you are thirsty for it, when you do not have it. True confidence is yours when your mind ceases to separate itself from itself. This heals the split between what you truly are and what you wrongly think you must become. The real you is composed of nothing but confidence.

Begin to see deeply. See that a completely rational mind does not need reassurance about itself from anyone. See that despair is nothing but a bluff, which self-insight can expose every time. See that unrenewed human minds cannot replace social chaos with social peace any more than a tornado can clean up the destruction caused by a previous tornado. See that we can feel that we are right without being right, but that we cannot be right without feeling right.

Slow down. Slow down everything—your thoughts and feelings and reactions and words and physical movements. Watch what happens. At first there will be slight discomfort, for mechanicalness always objects to a change of pace. Do it anyway. Slow down. Watch what happens next. You will see yourself in a new way; you will no longer take your fast ways as being good and necessary. You will catch a glimpse of what it means to be one with yourself.

THERE IS A WAY OUT

Mr. and Mrs. Fred F. said they sometimes felt pessimistic about erasing the past to start all over. They heard, "Insight into the problem and insight into our talent for self-rescue are always equal. If you know how to tie a knot in a length of rope you also know how to untie it. So pessimism is a wrong feeling because it is so impractical. Don't feel pessimistic over feelings of pessimism. Now you are practical people."

Any time you believe you are a permanent victim of your own negative thoughts, disbelieve it at once. Your free nature has power over confusion or rage or apprehension or any other harmful thought. Self-deliverance is free of time and space. It is as close as your own original mind. One way to return to this original mind is to not make connections where none exist. Maybe you cannot as yet see the way out. That has no connection with the fact that there is a way out.

In all the history of the human race, the truth has never rejected anyone. It accepts anyone who accepts it. It is just as much the permanent nature of the truth to accept everyone as it is the nature of light to shine. Therefore, to feel unworthy is simply one part of the entire nightmare caused by psychic hypnosis. No matter how terrible a person might be, regardless of his wrong deeds in the past, there is simply something he does not understand about his deeds, which is this: They were done by a hypnotized person who did not know he was hypnotized. When he snaps himself awake, he sees how accepted he is.

A hiking trail in a national forest was designed to provide hikers with sights of special interest, including an ancient cave and a gigantic tree. One group of hikers was disappointed at not finding these special attractions which they had read about. Upon returning to the starting point they discovered they had taken the wrong trail. It takes an intense honesty on our part to admit we have not found the inner attractions we have heard about. Many people hesitate to do this for fear there might not be a right trail after all. There is.

If you feel lost, simply remember that being lost consists only of not knowing what life is all about, of not realizing your true nature. There is nothing more to it than that, regardless of what guilt and fear and imagination try to make you believe. So be of good cheer. You are quite capable of recovering your true nature which understands life, so it is not at all necessary to feel lost. Do what must be done and you will surely find yourself. You are now learning what must be done.

TAKE THESE STEPS TOWARD NEW CONFIDENCE

1. Remain confident of entering the new inner world.
2. Use every experience for additional self-strength.
3. Your original nature cannot be frightened by anything.
4. Cosmic knowledge increases self-power quite natrually.
5. It is courageous to admit the need for deeper guidance.
6. Everything covered in this book is good news for you.
7. Use energy for self-exploration, and more energy will come.
8. The self-knowing person possesses permanent self-trust.
9. Authentic aid always appears to the sincere seeker.
10. Remember at all times that there is a way out.

Chapter 10

METHODS FOR ENDING
TROUBLE AND TENSION

A woman suffering from severe tension was asked to describe how she felt, to which she replied, "Crowded." That describes the condition of millions of people. They feel crowded by social pressure beyond their control, by the demands of relatives and employment and traffic, and most of all by their own colliding thoughts. You are now studying a system which relieves crowding completely, which provides you with endless open space.

Tension continues because we have not done for ourselves what can be done. All varieties of tension are caused by unawareness of our inner structure. The light of consciousness can abolish these causes, including contradictory desires, negative emotions and self-centered demands. We need not despairingly wonder how we are ever going to conquer these. We need only remember that the truth knows more about our tension than we do, then walk forward faithfully.

Tension is not caused by human conflict. Human conflict is caused by tension. All tension results from an individual's vain attempt to prove that an illusion is a reality. Whoever tries to prove his possession of a separate self apart from others will be tense, for it can never be proven. Out of this fundamental tension arises all other tensions, for example, a man thinks he proves his individuality by hurting another. He thinks, "I hurt him, therefore, I must be apart from him." What he does not see is his equal hurt while hurting another, which proves they are both the same.

Permanent relaxation comes as we relax our imaginary ideas about ourselves. We must remember that these imaginary self-images are always subconscious, unseen, so a man finds it difficult at first to connect his tension with them. Stated differently, a man cannot see how his self-pictures must always be at war with reality, causing endless tension and distress. It is his realization of all this which sets him free. To repeat, permanent relaxation comes as we relax our imaginary ideas about ourselves.

Al B., who had studied earnestly for six months, commented, "I am newly aware of the tension and exhaustion arising from defending myself and my ideas. May we discuss this?" Reply: "Question all ideas which you feel you must defend. The stronger your defense, the greater the need for questioning. You will find that these ideas are some of the bricks in your imaginary self-structure. In other words, you are defending your false self, which is harmful. The truth needs no defense. It can be explained, but never needs defense."

All human beings live under cosmic and universal laws, which exist both within and without their psychic systems. A man's task is to understand these laws in order to harmonize with them. For example, whoever understands the law of karma, of action and reaction, will not bring pressure upon himself by trying to put pressure on another.

YOUR NEW CURE FOR TENSION

Someone spoke up, "You say we must become aware of an unhappy state before we can get rid of it. What do you mean?" Reply: "Notice your tension when trying to please people from whom you want something. *Notice it.* That tension is all wrong. It is based on the mistaken belief that others can give you psychological rewards, such as consolation or excitement. Stop thinking that and all your human relations will be without tension. Now be aware of all this from now on.''

An ancient camel caravan in the Sahara approached an oasis with caution, for it had heard the rumor that concealed enemies were waiting. Coming close, the rumor was seen to be false, so the caravan entered into refreshment. Our psychological refreshment appears as we dare to draw close to those inner states which appear so alarming, whether that of panic or depression or perhaps an unidentified terror. So the invitation, ''Come close,'' takes its place as part of the cure, for the enemy disappears as consciousness appears.

It is the very fighting against life which produces the painful illusion that we need to fight life. Have you ever asked yourself exactly what or who you are fighting? A clear thinker will find no enemy anywhere. Incredibly, people fight in order to get rid of an enemy, not seeing that *their own fighting creates the appearance of an enemy.* All we need to do is to stop fighting, which makes the enemy disappear. What would happen if you simply ceased to fight? Find out.

Self-knowledge provides the necessary talent for raising unconscious thoughts up to consciousness. For instance, a man becomes conscious of his inability to become happier by changing his environment. At first this produces shock and despair, but now it is *conscious* despair, which makes all the difference in his world. By permitting the despair to reach its peak, it suddenly descends, like a hiker who passes over a hill-top. So the wise man never falls into despair over his despair, but uses it to abolish despair.

It is necessary to remember a basic rule about self-knowledge, for many people wrongly believe they understand themselves. The amount of self-understanding can be tested by observing the amount of self-concern. The more insight, the less concern; the less insight, the more concern. Any earnest person can use this helpful rule to prevent mistakes regarding self-understanding.

It is very strange. People think they can get rid of conflict by creating conflict. A nervous man reflects, "I am nervous, therefore, I will banish it by making demands on others." Now he is more nervous than before. A hostile woman thinks, "I am hostile, therefore, I will dissolve it by cultivating exterior friendliness." Now her self-division has increased her hostility. Both must realize that there is no "good self" which can reform the "bad self." When this is seen, they will give up illusory efforts, which permits reality to do its good work of ending conflict.

"It is starting to sink into my mind," testified Leonard M., "how we frantically defend the borrowed ideas which seem to protect us. It is dawning on me how they do the exact opposite; they keep us nervous. Will you please comment on this?" The comment was, "With the exception of the truth itself, there is absolutely nothing within you requiring protection."

HOW SELF-CORRECTION BANISHES WORRY

The manager of a motel commented, "Some people are afraid to examine these ideas for fear they will upset their lives." Response: "You mean their lives are not *already* upset? See how people are completely unaware of their slavery? A man looks at his frantic ambitions and proudly calls them creative actions. Something good would happen to that man if he would bravely face the contradiction between his proud labels and his actual conditions."

Your progress is helped by realizing that a first encounter with a new truth produces a crisis of one degree or another. When the new challenges the old, the old always shakes. Perhaps some time you will feel anxious over a new truth which seems a threat to your apparently secure position. In that case, just go ahead and be as anxious as you are, but keep studying, for that is the one thing anxiety cannot endure.

Do you ever feel overwhelmed by futility? What a profound teacher is futility! Nothing can tell you more of what you need to know. Listen carefully when something within you whispers, "There is a wrong way to live and there is a right way to live. The wrong way never works. The right way always works." Now, if life seems futile, that is really a friendly message informing you of the wrong way, the way that cannot work. See this much—see the wrong way as the wrong way that it is. Be aware of the wrong way, of futility, without feeling bad about it.

Any negative state, like worry, is like your shadow. If you run away, it pursues, but by standing still you see that it has no movement except that which you give it by running away. Remain steadfastly with what is called "disgrace" and the word loses its meaning, for "disgrace" is merely the opposite of "honor," and both are invented human notions. Declare, "I will not run away." You will now feel anxiety, but you will feel it consciously, for the first time, not unconsciously, as before. And consciousness is everything.

"Please explain," requested Max R., "the terrible tension we have over losing ourselves, I mean, we fear the loss of respect from others." Reply: "Social respect to and from others has no meaning whatsoever. It is all part of society's stage performance. The frightened actors and actresses have mutual contracts for keeping the drama going, to avoid facing their own emptiness. By leaving the stage, a man loses this fear, for only an actor worries over a bad performance."

Worry has no power except with the consent of the worried person. So we must examine how we unconsciously give consent to worry. A man who worries over business affairs has unknowingly connected them with false ideas about himself. With self-correction, words like "loss" and "failure" and "competition" lose their meanings to him completely. A mother who worries over her children must examine her own mind for wrong ideas about human life as a whole. She will then see clearly where she is responsible and where she is not, which brings total relief.

A class in Indiana was given this specific technique for understanding and ending mental discomfort: "When feeling uncomfortable, make yourself remember that you are in a state of psychic hypnosis of one form or another. This is always the case, though you may not see it. Remember this each time, for it twists the key which opens the lock.''

HOW TO END ALL FORMS OF FEAR

At her third appearance in class, Betsy Y. admitted her particular fear: ''I'm always worried that I might miss out on something. That may sound small, but it's a big bother.'' Comment: ''Yes, it's a common and often unrecognized anxiety, but it's like a man outdoors who fears he may miss the air. The false self, seeking impossible reassurances of its own false existence, is behind the worry. It makes people eager to be in on various activities, no matter how ridiculous they are. You don't have to be in on anything but your own deliverance.''

Nothing good can happen to an individual or to a nation as long as they are governed by fear, for fear is a barrier. The loved woman fears the sweet talk she has been hearing may soon be heard by another woman. The social reformer fears anyone who probes into his secret motives. And on and on. Fear is but one of the sour fruits of a mind which has not found itself. Fear is totally unnecessary, which is a fact known by a self-united mind.

As insurance against fear, people collect securities in the form of money, prestige, families, social activities and personal philosophies. They build as many separate little worlds as possible, so that if one fails, they still have the others. But they do not see that this process of pushing away fear is the very cause of fear, for it prevents the facing of fear, which could dissolve it. Consciousness is fearless.

Suppose you write the word *Home* on a slip of paper. A minute later, someone erases it. Does this make you feel insecure over the loss of your home? Of course not. You know that the word *Home* is merely an idea. This illustrates why people feel insecure over the loss of a friend or of employment or of other things. They simply have the wrong idea about the nature of security, so when reality erases a mere idea, panic appears. Friends and employment are real enough, but to depend upon them for security causes fear, for the idea is false. We can lose everything on the earthly plane, yet feel no loss on the spiritual plane.

To take a social position for yourself is to take a position against yourself. You cannot have a position on the social level without becoming a nervous hero to half the population and a nervous enemy to the other half. It is supposed to be a sign of strength and nobility to stand firmly on one side of a social question, but only a divided mind takes sides. A whole mind gets no false excitement in battling for this or that position, for it is its own unique position.

Separate yourself from the ways of the world. The world lives in fear. You need not live in fear. The world lives in pretense of being unafraid. You must not join this pretense. The world offers cures for fear. You must see that the cures are offered by the fearful. Separate yourself from the ways of the world, then fifty tons of worldly fear can fall and you will not feel an ounce.

A shipwrecked sailor found himself stranded on a desolate island, surrounded by a thick blanket of fog. Frantic efforts to build a raft ended in failure. Taking time to rest, he sighted through a hole in the fog another land. He set up a distress signal which was sighted on the other land and which brought rescue. When we relax from frantic efforts, we are able to see our source of rescue, which then arrives.

MAINTAIN A QUIETLY RECEPTIVE MIND

We must never try to merely relieve pressure, which is what troubled people often do, for example, by chattering or by getting emotional. Nothing profitable comes by trying to relieve pressure, though there may be temporary appearance of relief. Such attempts only transfer the pressure's hiding place, like a nervous fox darting behind another bush. But pressure can be ended by deeply understanding its false nature. This insight begins by studying pressure, which cannot be done if we try to relieve it.

The strain in a life can be clearly seen by observing the strain in daily speech. You can profitably observe this in both yourself and others. The observation produces awareness, and awareness ends strain. Suppose you notice your nervous strain when speaking with your superior at work. You have now caught strain in the act of robbing your energy. Next, realize that it is unnecessary to be afraid of any other human being. This insight erases strained speech.

A visitor from Denmark commented, ''I can see why we must become conscious of our confusion and anxiety, and I can see how it produces a healthy shock. But what prevents us from seeing ourselves as we are?'' Reply: ''The human game of playing it safe. We will never wake up by playing it safe. We must persistently venture outside our circle of pseudo-safety to where our notions can be battered by reality. You learn how to steer a boat in a storm by entering the storm.''

Think often about the value of right attitudes. One such attitude is consenting to let an unflattering fact about ourselves *be* a fact, with no concern for the way it punctures our delightfully flattering self-images. Such consent grows as we see facts as the healers they are, instead of the destroyers we feared. Take this winning attitude toward a tough problem: ''Regardless of everything, I intend to understand what this is all about.''

A discussion group with right attitudes is halfway out of the woods. The leader can read aloud the following reminder: ''We are here as men and women with a sincere wish to find the answers about ourselves. We set aside all of our acquired beliefs and opinions and listen with a quietly receptive mind to these higher truths. Our earnest intention is to catch a glimpse of something entirely new, something above the everyday mind, which will set us free.''

A somewhat timid student confessed, ''I am afraid of my own badness.'' Comment: ''We do not fear whatever we have conquered; we fear only that which, up to the present, has conquered us. An awakened man does not fear badness because he has conquered it through understanding. To him badness is neither a menace nor a disgrace; it is only a word describing a disadvantageous human condition. Awaken yourself, then you will be unafraid of human badness, you will handle it intelligently. Finally, by ending the fear of badness, you end badness itself.''

It is a superb act of self-elevation to constantly turn away from the old ways of thought and feeling. You don't have to understand the new ways in order to do this, and you need give no thought as to your strength and ability. You need only to deliberately turn your head away from all of the past. This turning spontaneously opens new scenes which become increasingly clear as you step ahead.

TENSION VANISHES THROUGH SELF-KNOWLEDGE

Beth G. asked, ''How can I remain at ease with people?'' Reply: ''Think of someone from whom you want nothing at all. Notice your ease toward him or her. Tension appears when you want something from another, perhaps security or agreement. You feel this person can fulfill you, but he cannot do so. Self-fulfillment abolishes the need to seek security from others, which makes you at ease with everyone.''

Tension does not arise when we ask the baker for bread or the salesman for shoes; we pay our money and are through with it. But ask for love and security and other psychological items and notice the arising of tension. This is because it is a wrong move, and our inner system is trying to tell us so. Why is it wrong? Because it is wrong for a tree to ask for the characteristics of a tree. Love, se-

curity, and all else are not separate from our true nature, and this is what we must see.

To go through your day unprepared is a marvelous
experience! I am not speaking of the necessary preparations for dinner or travel, but of preparations for present-
ing a desired image to others. Can you see the strain and
weariness of carefully preparing what you will say or how
you will act? See this, for most people don't. Such preparation must always be drawn from past behavior patterns,
therefore, it is fixed, stale, incapable of meeting each arriving moment with freshness and understanding. When you
are as new as each arriving moment—which you are, in
reality—all anxious preparation goes out the window. This
self-abandonment is the same as authentic self-control.

Man, with his frantic pursuits, is not really seeking to
get something, but to get rid of something. Haunted by
doubts about himself, Mr. A. tries to banish his doubts by
becoming rich and famous. Feeling lonely and insecure,
Mrs. B. attempts to push them away by involvement in
pointless activities. By seeing this, we turn our energies in
the right direction. We learn how to banish unhappiness in
the only way possible—through knowledge of the entire process of self-liberty.

People feel threatened and endangered by the outer
world. Why? It is easy to see why. A man who holds the
unconscious assumption that he must be the center of the
world's blessing will also feel himself to be the target of its
wrath. The first false assumption cannot exist without the
second. Where does the error begin? With self-centeredness. By imagining that he possesses a self which is apart
from the Cosmic Whole, he desperately tries to expand
and protect it—which always fails. How can the error end?
With the ending of the false self, which happens with earnest inquiry.

Earthly affairs are competitive, in which everyone frantically tries to win over everyone else, thus making it an
anxious earth. There is no such competition nor limitation in
the inner kingdom, so we must not permit the mind to see

the two as similar. The inner kingdom has no competition because there is no competitive mind there to create a feeling of rivalry. So no one need fear being left out, need not worry over having enough endurance to get his share. There are no shares. There is only the All. You are in that All.

Never mind if no one lets you in. The places they forbid you to enter or invite you to enter are places of secret heartache, but they know of nowhere else to go. They deny you in order to feel exclusive and they invite you in order to feel secure, but their terror remains. *There is another place.* Let this be your place. You can invite yourself into it right now. That is all there is to it.

HOW TO STOP FIGHTING LIFE

You can keep pressure out. Suppose someone is actually putting pressure on you. To whom does the pressure belong originally? To him, not you. Let it remain his pressure; do not unconsciously take it as your own. It does not become yours unless you permit it. If someone sets an unwanted sandwich on the table, you need not pick it up. This is an astonishing experience. The other man's pressure finds no one who wants it.

Inner progress can be compared to a drive from a noisy city to a peaceful countryside. At the start you are aware only of massive buildings and darting cars. Then, almost unnoticed at first, you see a single tree or a short stretch of wild grass. Gradually, you feel that something very interesting is happening, that something is changing. Heaviness is yielding to lightness, noise is surrendering to quietness. And the longer you travel the nicer it becomes.

What lightness is felt by whoever has no false desire for power over others! Kenneth S. felt this lightness. It took self-study, but he was tired enough of his heavy life to go to work. He broke through by observing his false pleasure in saying ''no'' to others, for the sake of feeling powerful. He testified, ''I saw both the childishness and the self-punishment in my behavior, which cleared it from my life.''

Both domination and submission are false steps taken by people in frantic attempts to feel secure. Domination, whether in the family or politics, is accompanied by the fear of losing power. Submission, whether to another's personality or to a religious doctrine, is accompanied by the sad sensing that one has somehow traded his inner integrity for the shiny beads of so-called security. You are not made for either domination or submission; you are made for yourself.

Because both domination and submission are false, a man quickly shifts from one to the other at the first sight of supposed advantage. We see this in a submissive prisoner who turns cruel and arrogant when overpowering his guard. A whole mind has nothing to do with these alternating states, which are only the exchanging of one anxiety for another. A whole mind is above these opposites, just as the moon is above the rising and falling tides.

If we are still fighting life, it is because we are not sufficiently tired of fighting. We have to get tired of fighting, but with an intelligent understanding of its futility, not with a feeling of despondency. This understanding comes when we no longer live apart from the Whole, when we no longer falsely assume that we have enemies.

One of the fine teachings of Epictetus can be summarized like this: ''When is a horse wretched? Not when he cannot fly, but only when he cannot run. When is a man unhappy? Not when he fails to achieve fame and fortune, but when he fails to be himself. You are not in this world to perform tasks which are opposed to your nature. You are here to merge your particular nature with all of nature.''

TRY THIS INTERESTING EXPERIMENT

A schoolboy was having trouble with an arithmetic problem. Helpfully, the teacher set a book on the baffled boy's desk, but returned a few minutes later to find the book unopened. The timid pupil explained, "I was afraid there might not be an answer." In your daily challenges, discover whether you may be saying the same thing unknowingly—and say it no more. Other people know the existence of the solution, and you can know it just as surely.

"In last week's class," said Lou B., "you said that psychological self-protection is pointless. I sense something here, but would like to hear more." Response: "There is no need to protect anything because there is no one to protect. The labels by which you identify yourself are not yourself at all, so protection is illusory and agonizing. Have you ever observed the tension in trying to protect what you call yourself? You can only see that there is nothing to protect by daring not to protect. Go ahead with this experiment. You will feel something very interesting."

The great human blunder lies in thinking that the so-called reasoning of the conditioned mind can solve human problems. The conditioned mind is the very cause of problems, and in no way can it rise above itself. Many people will not face this fact, for having identified with their conditioning, they fear its ending would be their ending. Its ending would be the very salvation they really want, but this will never be seen until they dare to see it. Only awareness of our conditioning can lift us above ourselves.

People timidly ask, "What is going to happen to me?" and then frantically search their conditioned minds for an answer. It is the attempt to answer the question by using memorized data which prevents awareness of the answer which exists only in the presently new moment. We must stick with the question without trying to answer it, which causes the question itself to disappear, so no answer is required.

Have you ever noticed the nervousness in waiting for something, even for something which you believe is good for you? Think about this for a moment, then realize that you need not wait for anything. There is nothing in future time for you because, in reality, there is no future time. The hope of fulfillment in the next hour or week or year will only divide you from yourself. Remain in the right time, which is now, and in the right place, which is with yourself. There is no tension in this time and place.

LET TENSION YIELD TO RELAXATION

1. You need no longer feel crowded by life's events.
2. The inner cause of tension is ended by self-understanding.
3. It is a fine feeling to be free of tense self-defense.
4. Refuse to consent to anxiety—and watch what happens.
5. See fear as a false and unnecessary emotion.
6. Instead of trying to relieve pressure, try to understand it.
7. Remember the value of maintaining positive attitudes.
8. Do not accept the pressures others try to put onto you.
9. Possess naturalness and we possess lasting relaxation.
10. Experiment with these ideas for abolishing tension.

Chapter 11

FASCINATING FACTS ABOUT THE RICHER LIFE

Lee K. said, "It is hard for me to find explanations for things I can't understand." Lee was told, "Look for the simple explanation; it is always there. The reason it is bad to have a self-image of being good is because it is merely an image and not a reality. The reason illusion is so painful is because it does not harmonize with our own nature. The reason we do not have schools for becoming mentally mature human beings is because qualified teachers are so hard to find."

One of the most persistent of errors is the belief that the spiritual life is separate from our daily life in the home or office. The truly spiritual mind sees no difference in the two. Differences in geography seem to make them different in psychology, but the wise mind sees them as one world. A businessman is doing spiritual work when he refuses to waste his energy in feeling disappointed. At the same time that Ralph Waldo Emerson was writing his victorious philosophies, he was also raising the best commercial apples in his home town of Concord, Massachusetts.

Before the sun rises, the world in front of you is a huge mass of blackness, broken only by vague and meaningless shapes. You cannot see connections between anything. But with dawning, the world takes shape, with everything in its right place, forming a connected whole. You see how a tree connects with the earth, how a white fence prettily surrounds a home. Our mental dawning reveals connected

143

completeness. We see how right-mindedness connects with gentlenss, how awareness makes us whole.

It is a peculiar tragedy that man spends his entire life doing two contradictory things: 1. Getting his mind on himself. 2. Getting his mind off himself. Chasing everywhere, he tries to attract favorable attention to himself, hoping to make his mind feel alive and important. But this means he must now work equally frantically at pushing away anything which threatens to expose the falsity of his aliveness. No wonder his days are nothing but wearisome worry. His task is to see that nervousness is not aliveness, for this will reveal true life.

We can never be for ourselves as long as we are against anyone else. To be against others is to be against ourselves. Take this as a spiritual teaching, but especially take it as psychological law, as scientific fact. Through wrong thinking, a man is first divided against himself, after which he projects his self-division into the outer world, thus falling into the false assumption that he is against the world and the world is against him. When this error is corrected, we are for ourselves at last, and we never feel that others are against us. Does this kind of life appeal to you?

Several members of a class in self-transformation complained to their teacher about the hardness of their lessons. The teacher addressed one student, "You mean it is *easy* living with your internal volcano which you admit erupts in panic so often?" Said the teacher to a second pupil, "You call it *easy* to fear the loss of affection from those you depend upon for affection?" Getting the point, the class ceased to complain.

HOW TO RECOGNIZE AN AUTHENTIC TEACHER

"I don't understand," said Edward B., "why the world continues to go wrong when the experts have so many corrective plans." Reply: "You cannot understand it because you cannot understand illusions; you can only see through them. The experts are always making plans, which are about as tremendous as secrets whispered between two small boys. See through yourself and you will see through everything else.''

Man's major social illusion is that he can build a society which is higher than his own psychological level. His illusory ideals blank out of his mind the man-made horrors before his very eyes. While gleefully waging war he piously preaches, "We must put an end to dreadful war." He believes he possesses an intelligence which is superior to his social environment, never seeing for one second that this environment is *himself*. Place man in paradise and he would soon reduce it to the level of his own frenzy.

We need the help of someone who knows more than we do. To find this person we must admit there is someone who knows more than we do. Human vanity, being the cunning creature that it is, tries to prevent this admission. Now, suddenly change everything. Forget about someone who can help you and remember that only the truth can help you. Now you will not get trapped by a dynamic human personality who only appears helpful—that dynamic human personality is afraid of the dark. Realizing all this, you now have inner guidance for finding someone who can truly help you.

One member of a study group remarked, "I have noticed a definite change in my feelings toward authentic spirtual teachers, including those of long ago, such as Lao-tse and Epictetus. I feel increasingly grateful and affectionate toward them." Comment: "Yes, this is what happens. Your receptivity to rightness is revealing itself. The truths they taught are becoming a permanent part of your nature. People should love the man who tells them the truth, regardless of how upsetting the truth may be. An authentic teacher is the best friend anyone can have."

Men who made cosmic discoveries of one depth or another have come from a wide variety of backgrounds: Leo Tolstoy: nobleman. Walt Whitman: schoolteacher. Baruch Spinoza: lens grinder. Henrik Ibsen: dramatist. Blaise Pas-

cal: scientist. Robert Browning: poet. John Bunyan: innocent prisoner. Ralph Waldo Emerson: clergyman. Carl
Jung: doctor. Soren Kierkegaard: philosopher. William
Blake: artist. Henry David Thoreau: businessman. Rene
Descartes: mathematician. Epictetus: slave. P. D. Ouspen-
sky: journalist. Marcus Aurelius: emperor. Arthur Schopenhauer: recluse. Hermann Hesse: novelist.

Here is how Alan E. began an interesting class discussion: "Suppose there are ten thousand men with reputa-
tions for knowing the truth. However, only one of them
really knows; the rest are self-deceived. How can a seeker
tell the difference?" Reply: "If you have even an ounce of
trueness in you, and talk with the ten thousand men, you
will sense and recognize the authentic teacher. Remember,
only trueness can recognize trueness, and it always does
so."

YOU ARE A NEW PERSON EVERY MOMENT

Some pupils of an Egyptian wise man asked him,
"How can we feel better? How can we have a happier
day?" The wise man replied, "*You* are your day. You *feel*
what you *are*. You feel your own character, your own level
of psychic maturity. You and your feelings are no more separate than water and its wetness. To change what you feel,
change what you are."

Making a decision about your marriage or career or
place of residence is nothing at all compared with your decision about your existence as a total human being. It is
strange how people fragment themselves with decisions as
a wife or as a businessman, never observing the whole life-
scene at once. Fall into the attitude that you can do nothing better for your entire life than to make affirmative decisions every hour. The decision to read truth-literature or
to contemplate are favorable decisions.

Ask yourself, "From what background am I getting
my responses to life?" Our quality of living depends upon
what we react *from*. A doctor reacts from his medical background to successfully treat a patient, but this is something

a lawyer cannot do. Our task is to build a mind from which we can respond rightly in all situations. Observe your next reaction and ask yourself, "What am I responding *from*?" The question can arouse energy for self-work.

When a truth is heard for the first time, it enters the mechanical part of the mind, which stores it up as memory. If it remains only in that section, it is never really understood, though a man may feel quite sure he has mastered it. He will then also mistake parroting for wisdom, which means he will say one thing but live by another. While living is certainly for learning, the time must come when learning turns to living.

A family made plans for visiting relatives who lived in a distant town in the mountains. Following the instructions in an old letter, they set out, only to lose themselves a half-dozen times. They discovered that the letter was too old to serve their present needs, for routes and roads had changed. Most people are unaware of how they travel today's road with yesterday's conditioning, and therefore cannot understand why they get lost. We can learn to travel with now-thinking, new-thinking, free from the old and useless routes of the past.

The correct role of memory is to store up practical facts for daily living. Unfortunately, we wrongly use memory to supply us with an identity based on past experiences. Do not let memory tell you that you are the same person at this instant that you were five minutes or twenty years ago, for you are not the same person. Identity does not continue from day to day, for time is an illusion. Buddha likened man's true nature to the flame of a candle which renews itself every moment.

Joyce H. said, "You say we can correct mistakes at once and forever. I would give anything to understand that." Comment: "Suppose you make a mistake which gets you into trouble with others. By working on it at once, according to these truths, you detach your false sense of self from it, which brings instant freedom. You see, the false self lives in time, so when this self falls away through insight, time vanishes, correction is immediate. It is an amazingly wonderful experience, which leaves no trace of guilt. This freedom provides wisdom for handling the other people with whom you were involved.''

HOW TO ATTRACT RIGHT ANSWERS

There was a magnificent temple in Tibet with twenty rooms of ancient statues and other classic works of art. Anyone could enter, but a new request had to be made each time in order to advance into the next room on the tour. This turned aside the mildly curious, but those with enough interest and persistence to make the twenty requests saw all the art treasures. "Ask and you will receive" is both a test and an invitation from higher places.

We can attract wrong answers or we can attract right answers. Follow this idea very carefully, for it has great depth. We attract wrong answers when we demand answers which are self-pleasing, which agree with our established beliefs. This changes nothing. But what happens if we make no demands? Obviously, we are left with our emptiness—which seems so frightening—but it is this emptiness which attracts right answers, for we have made room for them. This is what is meant by getting out of our own way.

On the everyday level it is sensible to try to predict how things will turn out, otherwise we get caught in the rain. But we must make no attempt to predict our psychological future, for such predictions will be based on memory, on the past, which will only mold the future according to the past. Prediction is anxiety disguised as excitement; it is a vain attempt to retain the so-called security of the known and the habitual. It interferes with the free flow of life, which is what we really want.

People go into these principles while hoping to secure certain benefits already judged as valuable and necessary. When seeing they are not going to get these selected prizes, a crisis arises. Genuine work begins after this crisis,

and the man who passes its test sees something both startling and healthy. He had no idea it would be like this,
and now realizes he would never have believed an en-
lightened man who might have described this new state.
But now he knows for himself, and he is not the same person he was before.

Alvin E. asked a question which has troubled mankind
throughout the ages: "How can I find God, Truth, Reality?" Response: "When you ask how *you* can find *God* you
have already divided your mind, which prevents discovery.
When your mind no longer thinks in the opposing terms of
you *and* God, you will understand. The first step is to see
how the use of words and labels create an appearance of division, but there is no division between you and God,
Truth, Reality."

All the great mysteries of religion become perfectly
clear to whoever pursues these principles to the very end.
Among them, you will understand what various scrip-
tures and legends mean by the "fall of man." In the simplest language possible, man's great blunder is his unconscious assumption that his *part* is the *whole*. Rarely does a
man perceive or admit it, but he firmly and falsely believes
he exists as a separate world which must battle and outwit
other separate worlds. Your own union with the Whole
ends the futile battle.

YOU CAN LIVE IN PURE DELIGHT

We cannot have an opinion about what is right. Rightness is never divided into opposing opinions; only wrongness is divided. A man can accept rightness or he can reject it, but he can never have an opinion toward it. A
man's attempts to have an opinion about rightness is an
evasion of rightness. A man who knows his way home has
no opinions whatever about the route.

The self-right man never sees others wrongly. Since his
psychic sight is not distorted by false self-interest, his view
toward others is clear, intelligent, practical. He does not

see a hostile or a conniving man as an enemy, but as a perplexed and anxious human being who does not know how
to escape his pain. He does not see an attractive person as
someone with charm or authority, but as someone whose
exterior brightness may indicate an interior emptiness. Self-
rightness never sees all this with self-righteousness; only
with compassionate understanding.

Said Eldon B., a Swedish student, "We are told to live
without self-interest, which is a puzzling teaching. How
can the self live without self-interest?" Reply: "First see
that self-interest is created by a false sense of self. Since this
self is artificial, so are its interests, but people never notice
this. Next, practice at giving up artificial interests. which
can be done by seeing how they cut off your true good.
You do not consist of the self involved in self-interest."

One of the purposes of higher truth is to make us feel
something we did not feel before. One such feeling is *delight*. Now, delight is entirely different from excitement. Excitement must depend upon an exterior source, like attending a party or meeting an attractive person of the opposite
sex. But delight is totally independent, for it exists as a
reality within yourself. If no one else on earth felt delight,
you could feel it. Have you not felt a new delight, perhaps
briefly, by absorbing these higher truths?

A dictator sailed to and invaded a distant land, carrying
back dozens of captives who were put to work in a village
near the sea. All day long the fresh sea breezes reminded the captives of their homeland. The dictator tried
every possible reward and punishment to make them forget,
but the sea breezes were overpowering. Captives of their
own dictatorial natures have the same reminder; nothing can
block it out. They must let it arouse inspired action toward
their rightful liberty.

A salesman asked, "How can we prevent ourselves
from falling under the spell of a negative atmosphere, as
when we are with upset people?" Reply: "You are always
your own psychological atmosphere. This means that when
you are upset by others, you also had a capacity for being

upset. But if inward reality keeps you calm, you can then impersonally observe an upset atmosphere without being a part of it.''

We must see how we unknowingly give other people power over us. If we resent another person's behavior toward us, we carelessly give him power to make us negative. If we react with gloom to a neighbor's gloomy remark, we permit him to tell us how to feel. Nothing prevents us from having total self-command, and nothing prevents us from having it right now.

WHAT YOU SHOULD KNOW ABOUT DESIRE

As you already know, some of your desires are fulfilled, while others are not. Perhaps you have wondered what determines the gain or lack of gain of a desire. A gain is not determined by a person's strong will-power, but by the alternating flow of nature which sometimes says *yes* and sometimes says *no*. Once you see that you do not determine events, a *no* cannot disturb you. We are disturbed only when *no* exposes our pretense of having a separate ego which can control events. You are not apart from the whole of nature, but are one with it.

Lew H. asked a familiar question: ''Why does life cruelly refuse me so many things I want?'' Reply: ''Who is this *you* who wants them? An acquired desire or hope or fear wants them, but you are none of these. You wrongly think a desire is *you*, which arouses false elation when the desire is won, or despair when it is denied. Mistakenly believing that a desire is *you*, you fearfully think your psychic survival depends upon getting it. This mistake causes all the horrors in the world. Think deeply about this until we go into it again.''

Other people are always telling a man who he is. He receives his descriptions through marriage and friendship, by social ties and business activities, by associating with like-minded people. But when other people tell him who he is, he is not at all who they say he is. The descriptions

may be pleasing and exciting, but they are powerless to establish his security, which he sorrowfully suspects. Only
the man himself can describe himself, which comes through
inner work, and which needs no confirmation from others.

It is an act of great intelligence to take a truth you cannot accept and try to see it as the fact it is. Take the fact
that you have never been cheated and never will be. Now,
everything within you may protest this fact, but it is still a
fact. The key to understanding lies in the word *you*. By
seeing your true identity as a person who is united with all
of life, not separated from it, you free yourself forever of
feeling cheated, no matter what happens to you.

In your natural state, you do not label yourself, which
is freedom. It is when we begin to apply labels that we
lose ourselves. In those rare flashes of spontaneity, which
children sometimes have, we do not know that we are either weak or strong, old or young, unwanted or popular.
Naturalness does not split itself into opposing labels; the natural man is one with himself and with everything else. We
do not lose ourselves until we believe society's false claim
that labels are realities. To save yourself, stop believing.

Because an authentic teacher is free from taking sides in
any human argument, he is not sought out by the general
public. The masses of people want to take a side on every
question because the agitation of quarreling with the other
side provides a false feeling of life. The true teacher thus
forces his hearers to come for the sake of the truth alone,
for the truth is above the foolish quarreling of both sides.
The curious masses crowded around Christ only until he
told them the truth, after which they "walked with him no
more." The question to every man is, "Do you want a
destructive position or do you want constructive truth?"

THE TRUE MEANING OF LOVE

The greatest moments in any man's life are those moments when he feels a pulsing of something he could not
feel before. It could be a new confidence in his mind to

keep him right as long as he keeps his mind right. It may be the astounding revelation of how much he secretly cherishes the very worries which he says he wants to banish. Perhaps it is a sensing of the existence of a totally new way to live, a way which excludes self-concern. These moments come with greater frequency and force to whoever wishes them.

One way to understand newness is to see life as a play in which the actors and actresses follow the script with monotonous precision. If heartache is written into the scenes, heartache will always be there as long as the players obey the static script. But life is not such a fixed drama; it only appears so because we do not question our mechanical roles. It is the never-ceasing questioning of things as they are which makes us original authors. You can rewrite the script to eliminate what you don't want and include what you like.

Everything works to your advantage as you do what must be done. You may not see this at first, in fact, you may feel that you are losing instead of gaining. *This loss is your gain.* See this! Your present life goes the way it does because you have certain ideas about it. Well, honestly, what kind of a life is it? If the life is wrong, the ideas in back of it are also wrong, so they must go. It is this loss of the harmful familiar that you feel. Don't love the familiar just because it seems comfortable. Love whatever is beyond the familiar, which is true love.

A park ranger wanted to know, "What is the meaning of the New Testament counsel to love our enemies?" Reply: "Unless love is truly understood, all kinds of troubles arise by distorting this counsel. Love exists only with the absence of the false sense of self, for this self cunningly calls itself loving in order to gain various rewards. It is very hard to see this at first, for the ego has a thousand masks for concealing its self-interest. True love exists when there is no self which likes to call itself loving. In this state, by the way, enemies do not exist."

One teacher of truth always startled a new class by

telling it, "The first rule is that you must never use the words *love* and *peace*. It is much easier to speak those words than to live their meaning. As long as you are satisfied with labels, you will never see the essence behind the labels. The word *gold* is not gold. I want you to *be*, not to quote."

An awakened man has very high standards which he will not lower one inch. Whoever wants what he has to offer may have it in abundance, but the seeker must climb upward. The ascending seeker must rid himself of his self-labels, such as being knowledgeable or authoratative. This lightening of himself enables him to reach the level of instruction, where he can hear and begin to understand his teacher. A sincere climber will never fail to hear.

Remind yourself every day that it is not enough to merely knock on the door of Truth—you must hammer on it. You must pound mightily, day and night, in storm and sunshine, insistent about it, without pride, always there, making it clear that you will not give up until you get in. The door begins to swing open the moment you have exhausted yourself.

HOW TO LOSE BURDENSOME DUTIES

Knowlege of the invisible world provides practical information about the visible world. In no other way can human affairs be understood and corrected, for only the higher can explain the lower, just as a parent understands a child. As an example we can take the connection between cosmic maturity and human fondness for noise. Noise serves as a distraction from the inner vacuum a person fears to face. With cosmic growth he is able to stop chattering so much, to let his muscles relax, to let his mind flow instead of explode.

A person who has ascended a step or two up the spiritual ladder sometimes worries over what he thinks are contradictions. He states, "One day I hear that an esoteric school is necessary, but the next day I hear that self-reliance alone can save us." He need not worry, for such contradictions exist only as long as he thinks from a divided mind. Mental division creates apparent contradictions, but when the mind rises above the stage of thinking in opposites, contradictions disappear. View the earth from the moon and you see one world, not opposing nations.

"I do not understand human gullibility," confessed Patricia A. "You say that consciousness alone can chase out our gullibility which brings grief. Please explain." Reply: "Unconsciousness of a particular weakness in ourselves makes us equally unconscious of it in another, making us his victim. Consciousness cures. When aware of the self-damage in hurting another, it stops, for we don't want to hurt ourselves. The light which makes us visible in our own home also makes the visiting neighbor visible."

If you belong to a club which you feel is giving you various benefits, you must contribute to that club. To remain a member in good standing, you must pay dues, obey the rules, and take on unwanted responsibilities. But if you lose interest in whatever the club offers, you no longer care about your standing, and you are free from burdensome duties. Mental freedom comes in a similar manner. If we intelligently lose interest in trying to impress others, we win instant liberation from dozens of expensive and unwanted duties. What burdens might you lose by doing this?

Progress can be illustrated by picturing a large rock on a hilltop. You want the rock out of the way, so you give it a push downhill. By the law of gravity it tumbles downward, but is eventually stopped by a tree. You shove it again, but this time it comes to rest on a flat area of ground. You persist with your part of the process, which permits gravity to do its part, until the rock reaches the bottom of the hill. Inwardly, your personal effort permits natural law to do its good work of removing difficulties.

REFLECT UPON THESE VALUABLE IDEAS

1. The mysteries of life can become clear to you.
2. Society cannot rise above its own psychological level.

3. Authentic teachers can help whoever is ready for help.
4. Permit self-renewal to do its good work every moment.
5. These ideas show you how to correct all kinds of errors.
6. See the difference between true and false values.
7. Pure delight is a result of living from your own mind.
8. Remain always within your own positive psychic atmosphere.
9. Review the principles in this chapter about genuine love.
10. You are now freeing yourself of burdensome duties.

Chapter 12

YOU CAN BANISH HEARTACHE AND PAIN

Someone requested, ''May we discuss a basic fact about suffering?'' Response: ''You suffer from the psychological level of misunderstanding which you occupy. Suffering continues as long as this level is occupied. For example, you may unconsciously believe that your past has power over your present, which is misunderstanding. Abandon a false love for both the pleasant and painful past and you rise above suffering.''

When you are out at night, you do not have any problems with the darkness, for you understand its nature. You do not try to hide from it, nor fight it with your fists, nor do you accuse others of trying to frighten you with darkness. Your understanding of the night frees you of problems that a small child might have with it. Now, apply this to psychic darkness. Realize that *the full understanding of psychic darkness is the very same thing as bright light.*

Let the following comment deepen your understanding. Suffering itself is not illusory, for whoever suffers from loneliness or apprehension suffers in fact. But suffering has an illusory cause, and since illusions can be dissolved, suffering can be eliminated. If you suffer from fear of losing someone or something, that is an illusion caused by not seeing the sufficiency of your own true nature. Take this comment and work with it, remembering that your real nature is free from distress.

When two separated facts finally meet they cause a

creative explosion—that of understanding. One day Lucy J. saw the fact of her own agony over the angry departure of someone she believed necessary to her happiness. The next week she saw a second fact—she had falsely valued this person. In this creative understanding, her agony vanished. You can connect any two facts from this book with equally fine results.

Pioneers in wild country used to build large campfires to keep back the strange creatures lurking in the surrounding darkness. Awareness is our bright light which prevents marauding thoughts from entering and injuring our inner self. As long as we keep the bright light burning, we have nothing to fear or to fight. Walt Whitman's awareness of this enabled him to declare, "Nothing exterior shall ever take command of me."

When you know what is truly right for you, self-harm becomes impossible. A truck driver who knows the danger of thin tires will never consent to driving on them. The very consciousness of danger prevents danger. It is the unconscious man who is a hazard to himself and others. Reflect upon this encouraging formula: Rightness can never act against itself.

HOW SELF-OBSERVATION ENDS SELF-STORMS

Leslie T., who worked as a food inspector for the county, brought up a point which had puzzled him: "It is said that we suffer because we live in mental movies, in imaginative films, made up from past experiences. Is this true?" Reply: "Of course it is, but you have never stood outside of yourself to observe it as an imaginative film. You *were* the film, instead of being an observer of it. So self-observation is absolutely essential, for it breaks the film, at first for a second, then ten seconds, and finally ends it altogether."

Do you think it is possible for you to look at your heartache with a calm and practical mind, just as you might stand on a cliff and watch an ocean storm? I assure you it is possible. You can separate yourself from an inner storm long enough to observe it with interest, instead of falling into its turmoil. This is how you change your relationship with the storm. By heedlessly falling into it, you become its victim, but by standing back and calmly watching, you become its conqueror. Go into action with this today.

The right intention turns unconscious suffering into conscious viewing. Perhaps we suffer from humiliation. Now, humiliation is a clear announcement of wrongness somewhere. Our response determines whether we sink or rise. A refused humiliation must remain on the mechanical and unconscious level, where it will repeat itself endlessly. But if it is received with the intention of understanding it, we now suffer *consciously*. This raises the humiliation to the level of awareness, which means it will no longer repeat itself.

Risk rejection at every opportunity. That is how to break out of yourself. We learn from rejection, not from acceptance. Look at yourself this very moment to see the nature of your mental defenses. Realize that defenses defend nothing; see that the walls we erect for keeping out so-called enemies are the same walls which keep us in. Start in small ways to risk rejection of your favorite ideas, while quietly watching how it affects you. Such observation-without-comment breaks down walls and lets you out to play.

We can illustrate the difference between a hardened mind and a free mind. Toss an egg into the yard and it will smash itself against whatever it strikes. But a tossed rubber ball bounces off all objects without harm to itself. A hardened mind, by its own insistence upon hardness, sets the stage for its own shattering. Whenever a demand meets a *no*, something cracks. But by observing its own process of suffering, this hardened mind could begin to see why it happens. Then, seeing itself as the illness, it also sees itself as the doctor. That is self-softening, self-awakening.

A father took his small son for a walk across a high bridge. Halfway across, the unusual height frightened the boy, causing him to huddle close to his father. "Come along," the father assured. "We will go beyond it." A frightening problem is solved by going beyond it. To go beyond does not mean to run away, but to understand yourself, for the problem and the person with the problem are one and the same. To fight a problem on its own battleground is useless; it can only replace an old crisis with a new crisis. You are your own solution.

THE CURIOUS TRUTH ABOUT REVELATIONS

A group of new students entered the hall, eager to hear the first words of their teacher, which were, "Mankind is caught in a dreadful trap. That is a fact. Do not deny the trap and do not try to explain it away. Simply see that you are *personally* in that trap. Now you are ready for another fact, which can be given in a single sentence. If you have a deep enough desire to get out of the trap, you can do so." With this, the teacher left, leaving the students in a thoughtful mood.

Where is the headache? The headache is within the person suffering from the headache. So where must he look in order to understand the headache? Within himself. A basic cause of his headache is his belief that the unnecessary is necessary, for example, that he must prove himself to others. But whatever the cause, the cure cannot come by blaming others or by generously supplying aspirin tablets to other people with headaches. The man with the headache is the one who must look to and cure his headache.

The trouble is, many people take the healing truth as a personal insult. A sufferer comes for help and is told, "Your self-centeredness must be abolished." He never returns. Man has everything exactly backward. He takes rejection of the true as the way to avoid self-destruction, and takes acceptance of falsehood as the way to life. With the courage to reject falsehood, even in small ways at first, we catch a glimpse of our life-damaging error. From that point on we begin to truly save ourselves.

Imagine a lonely native of an isolated island who knows nothing about other lands. Believing his own world to be the only one which exists, he will fight anyone who tries to remove him from what he believes is his security. His fear for his safety is an illusion, but his defensiveness prevents awareness from exposing the illusion. In order to see, he must venture. Here you have a grand summary of man's basic problem and its solution.

Everyone wants lovely revelations, but few people want upsetting shocks. In this new approach to life, you must see a revelation and a shock as the same thing, which they are. A shock is like a friend who disturbs your beautiful daydream to shout warning of the slippery street just ahead. The secret of success is to see a shock as a revelation of some new benefit. When a revealing shock is accepted fully, it ceases to cause shock, for then there is no difference between the conscious mind and the unconscious mind.

When people meet higher ideas for the first time, they ask themselves many questions, for example, "Why is it more advantageous to study my inner nature than to study ways to get ahead in the world?" Or they ask, "Why is it better to spend time learning what life is all about instead of simply enjoying life as it comes along?" There are many answers, but here is just one: Why is it better to be an awakened human being than to be a human being who only imagines he is awake? Because in a crisis, the imagining man cracks up, while the awakened man walks right through it.

BREAK THE CHAINS OF THE PAST

Lester D. finally admitted the cause of his despondency, saying, "Through my own foolishness I missed several opportunities for making something of

myself. How can I get another chance?'' Response: ''You
have missed nothing. Stop believing in words. You
connect the word *opportunity* with the false belief that you
must make something of yourself. End the torture. There
is no such thing as this or that opportunity for you; there
is only the whole unfolding life, which includes the whole
unfolding of you.''

In reality, distress has no moment to moment hold on
you. We feel the chain of distress because of the illusion
that we live in time. We assume yesterday must repeat itself today, and it is that very wrong assumption which
causes the repetition of distress. You can break the chain
any moment you like. Children may feel distressed, but
they laugh the next moment because the artificial self-
structure, which lives in time, has not as yet hardened.
Self-melting frees us of time and its distress.

Picture two men walking through a recent battlefield,
surrounded by silent reminders of man's horror toward
man. One viewer is frightened by the shattered steel and
black smoke, but the other walks in self-possession. It is
this way in life. Most men stare in horror at their own
deeds, for they know they will do it again. But the man
who has learned to possess himself walks through life with
understanding of it all. Having ended his own unconscious
need for fighting, the war has ended for him forever.

You are never pained by what happens to you; you are
pained by your thought about what happens. Here is the
open door to liberation which man fails to enter because he
does not exercise his powers of understanding. Understanding could begin by refusing absolutely to complain about
what he calls injustice. This refusal would reveal how
much he secretly loves complaint, for without its agitation
he would feel dull and unimportant. But when complaint
disappears, so does the pain of feeling treated unjustly.

Society has its rules covering eligibility. Certain requirements must be met if one is to be eligible for the school or
the employment or the pension. Reality has its own rules
for eligibility into the kingdom. If you see how your fierce

clinging to your present philosophy has given you nothing but secret heartache, you are eligible for the true philosophy. If you are aware that you have not found contentment in the kind of life you are now living, you are eligible for a new life.

Mr. and Mrs. Leon G., who led a weekly study group in Texas, used these principles for several discussions: 1. It is the spiritual life which is logical, and the worldly life which is illogical. 2. Nothing can take away our liberty to know the truth. 3. In a society of thousands of illegitimate objectives, our right objective is self-contentment. 4. The answer to all problems lies within ourselves. 5. Consciousness is the only influence which is right and beneficial for us.

WISELY USE SORROW TO END SORROW

A teacher of mysticism taught his class, "A rejected or an insulted man feels a peculiar thrill from the experience. To find true life, you must refuse the false pleasure resulting from rejection or insult. At first you will feel vacant, but it is the vacancy of a field cleared of weeds. Now you can plant something fruitful."

There is no virtue in suffering. In itself, suffering has no value and no reward. This is contrary to what confused people like to believe, for suffering fills a place inside them which would feel empty if it were not agitated by pain. Suffering is caused by self-contradiction, and there is no virtue in contradiction; there is only a need for correction. The only wise course to take with suffering is to use it to end it.

True love and true conscience come to a man when he ceases to enjoy his sufferings which make him the center of his own attention. The energy with which he enjoys his self-hurt is the same energy used to hurt others; the two always go together destructively. It is psychological law that a man always treats others exactly as he treats himself, though he rarely sees it. It is the voluntary abandonment of cherished suffering which creates true love and conscience.

When a man is afraid of another man or of a circumstance, his first thought is to get rid of the threat. He almost never thinks in any other way toward his problem. Threats appear so often that he sometimes wonders how he can keep his sanity, yet he never asks himself why they continue to appear. He can cure himself by reflecting, "Maybe I have threats in my life because my own mind has created them in some way. Maybe there is a connection between me and what happens to me that I do not see. Well, I'll investigate."

One way to escape the trap of unhappiness is to consistently suspend feelings of excitement which try to invade you. Excitement is imitation happiness, and therefore no happiness at all. Glance around and you will see millions of excited slaves. Suspend the excitement which tries to enter when you win a success of some kind. This interrupts the mechanical pattern long enough for newness to slip in. On the other side of rising and falling excitement is lasting happiness.

"In keeping with your request for direct questions," said Hugo T., "how can any person free himself from inner pain?" Reply: "There are only two ways to live. If a man will not listen to his own inner reason, he will have to listen to his own inner pain. He can choose either teacher. This is why I have urged you to get tired of suffering. Listen to reason and you will no longer have to listen to pain. This is the entire story."

If you bend a strip of metal back and forth long enough it will get tired and break. Similarly, mental miseries have a breaking point at which they get tired and break away from us. Our task is to continue the esoteric exploration until this point is reached. It will surely come, whether the problem is that of indecision, of feelings of futility, or of an inability to understand yourself.

ACCEPT THIS INVITATION TO REST

Charlotte J. requested, "May we hear of a practical way to think toward a blunder? We seem to make a second blunder when trying to think our way out of a first one." Reply: "Think of a blunder as you would think of a boat in a wheat field—it just does not belong there. Don't get panicky over a mistake; just see it as being unnatural to your true nature. That is corrective thinking."

A driver for a furniture company was instructed to drive an empty truck to a warehouse and pick up a load of chairs. Getting his orders backward, he loaded his truck with chairs and delivered them to the warehouse. The same thing happens when spiritual orders are misunderstood. Instead of performing free actions we carry pointless burdens. Do you know people burdened with rigid minds or oppressive ambitions or sullen behavior? They are carrying needless burdens.

The sorrowful and the burdened are often invited to come to rest. Another invitation, heard less often but equally gentle, is extended to the angry and the bitter. Anger is just as great a burden as sorrow. This kind of pain exists only because there is something which is not understood. The intelligent action is to refuse to be engrossed with the pain and to energize oneself toward the needed insight, which brings rest.

Self-knowledge provides self-unity. Self-unity provides self-contentment. Self-contentment has nothing to do but enjoy itself. John Newton summarizes, "If two angels were sent down from heaven—one to conduct an empire, and the other to sweep a street—they would feel no inclination to change employments."

How unknowing we are if we try to prevent natural change in our life, and how much we suffer needlessly. Since the very nature of the universe is change, our efforts to remain in familiar places can only frustrate us. You and your world are one. Let yourself remain in oneness, never

165

fighting change, and watch your world become new. In taking an airplane trip around the world, you may change airplanes several times, but you still remain one with the flight. Life is like that.

A pupil requested, "Please explain what you mean by mechanical thinking." Reply: "If you call on a friend with a package in your hand, he will sight it at once and will usually assume or hope it is a gift for him. His mind mechanically believes that everything should revolve around his personal interests. He is unaware of this and would deny it if told about it. This is mechanical thinking, which is painfully self-centered."

The senses are pure channels. Eyes and ears in themselves cannot be affected by what is called either good or bad news. Division into good or bad is made only when an impression reaches the mind. The mind interprets everything as either good or bad according to its own preferences and self-interests. The mind which operates above the level of acquired preferences makes no divisions of good or bad. This wise mind sees everything, understands everything, and is disturbed by nothing.

THINK ABOUT THESE PROFOUND TRUTHS

One of the most painful questions a human being asks is, "Why can't things turn out the way I want?" The answer is available to the daring. The question itself is false, for it mistakenly assumes the existence of a separate self which is opposed by events and by other people. To say "I" is to create an opposing "you", which makes conflict inevitable. Let insight dissolve this false belief in a separate self, let insight lead to Oneness, then both the question and its pain disappear.

Every genuine human need has a fulfillment. God, Truth, Reality, can no more fail you than water can fail to satisfy thirst. But we must work to recognize a false need when we see one. A hypnotized man might seek food for an imaginary cat, but upon awakening he stops seeking.

You do not need to seek an identity for yourself through human labels or through worldly success. You do need to see the uselessness of such seeking. The very seeing of this uselessness is your fulfillment.

An archeologist in Egypt discovered a statue which appeared to represent an ancient pharaoh. With great care and trembling, he supervised the packing and shipping of his statue. And with great relief he saw it complete the sea journey from Egypt to the United States. But as the statue was being hauled up the museum's steps, it crashed, leaving only unshapely pieces. In great pain, the archeologist examined the pieces, to discover that the statue was a hoax, a fake—which ended his pain. When your life shatters, examine the pieces. Sharp sight will reveal a hoax—which ends your pain.

The illusion a man cherishes above all others is the illusion of having a separate self which is apart from the whole of life. To perpetuate this illusion, he fights, for fighting appears to create a separate self, a self with an opposite, an enemy. So human beings fight and then tell lies about their reasons for fighting. Whether in family quarrels or in worldwide wars, this destructive process works the same way. If you want out of the battle, understand all this. Remember, it is the fighting itself which creates the illusion of the need to fight. If you simply stopped fighting, where would be the need to fight? Nowhere.

People hesitate at the door to higher truth for fear of losing something. It is utterly fantastic. A miserable man thinks he will lose his happiness! A hard and bitter woman thinks she will lose her lovely personality! Do you see how their illusions about themselves block their way? So a preliminary insight is to see that we have nothing to lose but our suffering.

"What mistake do others make which we must guard against?" asked Dorothy U. Answer: "Guard against a fickle interest in your own deliverance. People will listen intently when informed that there is a way out of suffering,

but when told they must banish their misconceptions of
themselves, they hesitate. So maintain an enthusiastic interest in your own enlightenment, regardless of where the
path leads you.''

THE CURE IS NOW AT HAND

Eastern history tells of a wealthy individual named
Yasas. For years he had power to command every desire
for luxury and pleasure, including the company of beautiful women. But his heart was weary with the emptiness of
it all. During one evening of great sorrow he wandered
into the Deer Park where Buddha was meditating. Yasas
knew instantly that this splendid human being before him
could show him the way out of suffering. From that evening forward, Yasas was a loyal disciple of truth. The
lesson: When we are weary enough of artificial living, we
will find an authentic teacher.

The reason a teacher can help others is because his insight is not blocked by society's labels and titles and reputa-
tions. He never sees a famous statesman or a wealthy businessman or a glamorous woman. He sees straight through
human labels, as if through glass, to see the inner person
himself—and what he sees is a frightened and confused human being. If that frightened person is ready, the teacher
can help him.

If you look at a half-finished house you are building,
you do not condemn its unfinished condition. You do not
call it inferior to another house, nor do you get panicky
over its appearance. All you do is realize its need for additional work. Think like this toward yourself. Whatever
your present condition, just realize the need for more
construction. Be patient toward yourself, but also be quite
firm toward the necessary work.

Richard W., one of a study group, said he knew
nothing about the nature of mental anguish. Along with
the rest of the class, Richard was told, ''Yes, you know.

When told that almost all your suffering is done in secret, you know that is a fact. Your feelings know all about anguish, but you fail to take time to learn the cure. The cure is not *away* from the suffering, but right in the very center of it. Your cure is at hand right now."

What can keep us right in any situation? Author Berthold Auerbach replies, "Above everything, you must command yourself, and your true self is not your wildly roving thoughts." You can maintain self-command in any difficulty by saying, "There is something here I do not understand as yet, but I intend to do so." People always forget that a rocking boat can still be rowed.

FOREMOST FEATURES OF THIS CHAPTER

1. Correct our misunderstandings and we correct our pains.
2. Awareness is the perfect guard against costly mistakes.
3. We must study suffering, and not attempt to avoid it.
4. Remember, the solution to sorrow resides within your mind.
5. Unhappy experiences can be used to abolish unhappiness.
6. These ideas make you eligible for a new contentment.
7. The ending of suffering is the beginning of true love.
8. Sorrow soon leaves the person who has no use for it.
9. Have a persistent interest in the ending of heartache.
10. The cure you want is now ready for your taking.

Chapter 13

ACTIONS FOR WINNING PRACTICAL REWARDS

People exclaim, as did Gene M., "But I just don't know what to do!" It was explained to Gene, "If you are sitting in a dark room in the early morning, your very awareness of the darkness tells you what to do—open the curtains and admit sunlight. Your mind works as a whole unit, seeing both the cause of the darkness and its cure at the same instant. So right action in any situation is to become totally aware of it. This is not a mysterious process; you can do it."

What is right action? True action and true understanding are the same thing. Knowing *is* doing. A small child asks his mother for a glass of water, so she hands him a glass filled with ice cubes. Puzzled and annoyed, the child protests. His mother explains that ice and water are the same thing in different forms. The child now understands he has nothing to do but let nature perform her perfect work. Realize that you and nature are the same thing in different forms, in one, undivided whole. Then, your knowing is your perfect action.

A legend tells of a city in which everyone was at peace with himself and with others. The city was surrounded by a deep gorge which had no permanent bridge over it. Any individual who wished to reach this happy land had to build a bridge with his own hands. Those with a deep desire to cross over, succeeded in doing so by busying themselves with ropes and boards. That is the kind of enthusiastic self-reliance by which we cross over from the psychic land we now occupy.

Many people unconsciously associate activity with physical and public movement only, which blocks insight into true action. We are more than physical movement, so to satisfy the physical body only is to leave the rest of us unsatisfied. Maybe you have observed people who are mentally limp and dependent, who wait eagerly for the slightest event or remark to supply them with something to think about. A whole man does not live in such boredom. He is always on the move in one way or another, expressing the pure action of his complete self.

Artificial actions result in artificial rewards. An artificial action is one performed without understanding the personal motive behind it. Take what society calls good works. Such good works are often done in public with the unconscious motive of attracting applause, or from the vanity of giving to others. Meister Eckhart declared, ''Visible deeds do not increase the goodness of the inner life, no matter how numerous.'' A man with artificial goodness can bring you candy in the hospital, but the man with cosmic goodness can show you how to stay out of the hospital.

In tracking down the better life, be like a detective on a case. A detective never prejudges anyone as guilty or innocent, but lets the facts lead wherever they wish. Suppose you feel that others take advantage of you, so you gather various clues about the situation. That case will then be solved by seeing that there is no way whatever to take advantage of a free man.

METHODS FOR BENEFICIAL ACTION

A visitor to a city happened to find himself at the edge of a crowd which was honoring a local citizen. The visitor asked the nearest man what the citizen had done to deserve the honor, to which the man replied, ''He writes both good and bad poems.'' Asked the visitor, ''Why don't you just honor him for his good poems?'' The man answered, ''We can't—no one knows which is which.'' That is how the world acts. Few know the difference between the real and the unreal, but everyone acts anyway, with disastrous consquences.

When people don't know the one right thing to do, they try to make it up by doing a thousand wrong things. But a thousand zeros still add up to zero. Think of one thought of quality today, just one, and that one will be yours, not society's. Think of the folly of an unexamined life. That is quality. Think of those inner whispers which declare, "There is another way." That is quality.

Hold every thought and action up to the light of the question, "Does this increase my agitation or does it suspend my agitation?" After doing this you can make a great decision in your favor. You can decide to no longer enjoy agitation. Yes, the enjoyment of agitation and sensation is the nervous life of most people. Whoever screams back when screamed at enjoys his screaming. Agitation is false life, so you will decide in favor of true life by no longer paying the dreadful price of agitation.

The individual who no longer wishes to go along with his own pain will run into many new experiences which at first will seem discouraging. For example, in his uncertain search he will meet many false prophets and senseless systems. Fortunately, he can learn something even when temporarily attracted to them. By keeping his eyes open he can see that the ideas given him do not really change anything on the inside; they merely distract him from his despair. Then, like the wise albatross which refuses to alight on a sinking ship, he will finally fly all the way to solid ground.

Spencer M. commented, "You said we are made safe by seeing what we do not presently see. Will you please explain?" Reply: "A man on a camping trip sets up his tent at night in a convenient spot. The next morning he is shocked by seeing a sign prohibiting camping in that area because it is next to a steep cliff. Awareness of higher laws brings safety. Think of a mistake in the past which you no longer make. Why? Because you are conscious of its harm."

In order to see what must be seen, we must slow

down. Rushing through life is like being in such a hurry to finish reading a book that we skip every other sentence. Neither a book nor life can be understood like this. We must not merely be aware of each successive moment, but must be *in* each moment, which makes life make sense.

One rich result of these studies is the ascending ability to take everything in the right way—the right way being that which is right for *you*, not for your habitual ideas. Where you formerly resisted distress, you now take it as a message about a freedom which awaits you. Where you formerly wondered about conflicting teachings, you now understand that all authentic instructors teach the same One Truth, though in their own words.

HOW AWARENESS CREATES RIGHT ACTION

Do not anxiously feel that you do not have enough time to find yourself. Time has no claim on you whatever. Deliverance is now, for that is the only time there is. A decision to change yourself tomorrow is no decision at all. Just ask yourself whether you want to remain caught in the surrounding social madness, and if you don't, start now to break away.

We must experience life purely. To understand what this means we can observe the nature of impure experiences, which are self-contradictions. A man who craves public admiration will have to pretend to like many people he really dislikes, which divides him against himself. A woman seeking excitement in buying new clothes inwardly senses how soon she must return to her emptiness, which makes it an impure experience. We experience life purely when we are one with ourselves. This pure singleness starts by honestly observing self-division.

"You have stated," said Everett F., "that simple awareness produces truly intelligent action. May we have an example of such action?" Reply: "If you became clearly aware of the inner agony of people in high social and political positions, you would gladly trade all such posi-

tions for an evening's conversation with a few friends about
the meaning of life.''

You can make an interesting experiment with a surprising point. Are you aware of the tone of your own voice?
Have you every consciously listened to it? Do so right
now. Speak aloud and be aware of the tone of your voice.
Perhaps you hear it as high or low, soft or heavy. Do you
see your awareness of something which has been close to
you for years but which you may not have noticed before?
This is not merely a stunt. This awareness is the same
awareness which ends feelings of futility and which makes
you indifferent to what others think of you.

The unawakened man can attend only to his own
business, which is his self-centered prison, but which he assumes is the entire and only universe. Though appearing
interested in others, cunning self-interest is his only motive. But the aware man has an amazing mind which truly
spans the whole universe, for he does not divide it into
''yours and mine.'' While handling his own affairs efficiently, he has deep insight into the ways of suffering men.
He could tell them about the real world—if only they would
listen. He is truly a wise man, though few know it.

The reason an unknowing man can get very little from
an authentic teacher is because the unknowing man does
not know that the teacher knows. To know a diamond when
you see one you must already know something about
diamonds. So it is vital for the seeker to first make a
personal effort toward self-enlightenment, after which the
teacher's expanded light can be recognized and received.

Almost everyone has the feeling that their activities, no
matter how exciting or successful, lack something. This
feeling never arises when you work enthusiastically with
these principles, for you are working with dynamic forces.
Then, whatever you do, you do something for yourself, for
you are observing, noting, understanding, possessing.
With great pleasure you see the similarity between these
ideas and silver coins, for both retain their value in all
kinds of climate.

SAIL THE UNKNOWN PSYCHIC SEAS

"Explore the unknown!" That is the counsel of self-liberated teachers. When people fear the unknown they quickly direct their hostility toward it. So to them the unknown remains a source of terror instead of healing. The free man declares, "I want to show you how everything can be made right, so please come with me into an amazing exploration of the unknown."

The valuable unknown first appear to us as a shock or a bewilderment. Because the habit-heavy mind is unable to recognize or classify a new experience, because it is unable to fit it into any of its familiar and comfortable pockets, it becomes uneasy. It is like suddenly discovering a secret closet in a home you have occupied for many years. The wise individual never turns aside from his bewilderment before the unknown, but consciously observes its passage through his mind. This prevents the unknown experience from turning into a negative feeling, perhaps dread or defensiveness.

Gerald B. began the conversation, "It is inspiring to hear you say we can call the bluff on whatever frightens us, for example, domineering people. Emerson remarked that society is fiercely against anyone who tries to regain the natural independence of his mind. Will you please comment on this?" Response: "Society's task is to make a mindless machine out of you. Your task is to refuse to be a machine."

Decide today that you will no longer be bluffed by anyone. This is an essential step to self-freedom. Watch what happens the next time someone frightens you. Realize first of all that you have wrongly permitted him to influence you. Then, look at that other man. Look at him and remember that a hard and angry look is nothing more than the pathetic bluff of a frightened human being.

Wishing to improve their health, a group of people set sail for a distant island where everyone was said to be perfectly healthy. But many passengers left the ship at various ports along the way. Some explained that they yearned to return to their familiar country, others complained of the ocean storms, while others said they had found new interests. But one passenger, who had an intense wish for fresh health, reached the island, to find it as delightfully healthy as had been described. The lesson: Never mind what others do with their lives; do what is right for your life.

Bewildered people say they do not know what to believe. Wonderful! There is hope for whoever does not know what to believe. Human belief is a combination of superstition, gullibility and mental laziness. We need not believe anything; we need to find, to see, to know. A ship tied to the dock cannot explore new lands. A man tied to his beliefs cannot see anything beyond them. This is why the Zen masters call out, "Let go!" How do you let go? You just let go.

Have no fear of sailing the foggy seas within you. The harbor is beyond the rocks, but you must not imagine what the harbor is like, for then you will reach only an imaginary harbor. Enter the fog, for the navigator within you knows the way. Enter the fog, remain in the fog, and when it lifts you will find yourself beyond the rocks and within the harbor.

HOW TO END INJURIOUS ACTION

What kind of man performs right action all the time? The man who is one with himself, whose acts are not opposed by his feelings, whose words are not different from his thoughts. His unified inner state *is* his action, and it is always healthy action. Being one with everything, including the exterior world, nothing can oppose or harm him. If you are deeply interested in living like this, it can be done.

Remember, a refusal to engage in self-hurtful action comes in one way only—by a clear recognition of hurtful action *as* hurtful. A child who finally connects a hurting toe with his careless bumping of that toe becomes cautious. Our awareness of cause and effect in self-injury ends our participation in it. Consciousness breaks the chain of cause and effect. For example, it is against anyone's true interests to feel dejected when criticized, for you must study the feeling, not surrender to it.

Forrest G., who managed a ranch, expressed his bewilderment about a certain point: "If so much of our energy is directed toward inner items, won't it distract us from outer necessities, such as our employment?" Response: "Why do you divide life into the inner and the outer? They are the same. Inner efficiency supplies outer efficiency in employment and in everything else."

As long as a man does not see what is right, he will do wrong. Because man's inner crisis is so fantastically severe, no suggestion for relief is too fantastic to be tried. A man somehow connected with a sensational human tragedy which does not harm him personally can hardly believe his good fortune. At last he has an intense distraction from the tragedy of his own life. And when it is all over, he sits sadly at home to wait hopefully for a friendly knock on the door. He listens for the wrong visitor.

Self-awakening is the one great task of every man and woman on earth. To be self-awake is to be free of unconscious self-sleep. The first step toward self-awakening is to detect one's actual state of psychic sleep, which is characterized by secret suffering, fear, anguish, and similar negative states.

Suppose an electrical failure in a large factory changed the clocks so that they all showed a different time. There would be considerable chaos if every employee scheduled his work according to the clock he happened to see. But, if everyone went by his own watch, all would be well. The social scene is like that. People schedule their lives according to accidentally-absorbed ideas, never considering that the ideas might be contrary to their own best interests. This is why Socrates repeatedly advised, "Inquire!"

It is necessary to inquire with the right intention. If you get lost while trying to reach a certain destination, perhaps a friend's home, you may ask a stranger for directions. However, you do not ask whether the road is new

or smooth; you ask whether it is the right road. We must
not ask whether a spiritual teaching is exciting or popular,
but whether it is true.

THE PERFECT SENSIBLENESS OF THESE IDEAS

Correct action is action against anything which is *wrong,*
not merely against whatever is wrong with the neighbor or
the social system. It is an endless trick of egotism to see
wrongness outside of itself, while conveniently forgetting
its own falsity which contributes to the very social system
it denounces. By seeing both sides of wrongness at once,
both within and without, we no longer divide it, which
means we are no longer wrong.

How sensible it all is! Since we make mistakes because
we unconsciously judge people from exterior appearances,
what perfect sense it makes to probe deeply into human
nature. Since no man can act higher than his level of understanding, the only sensible thing for him to do is raise
his psychic level. Since people are afraid of losing the
game, what wonderful sense they show by realizing that
the game itself is false.

A citizen was weary of the strife and terror of his land,
so he decided to emigrate to another country. When asking
others for the right ship to take, he was directed to several
harbors. Upon arriving at the shores he found no ships at
all, which caused him to doubt the very existence of a
right ship. But urged on by deep desire, he located and
boarded the right ship. Here is a right ship for you: There
is something in you which is capable of not being the usual
you.

Have you ever felt that there is much too much of yourself in everything you do? Have you ever sensed what a relief it would be to cut loose from that person who so
frantically tries to push and plot and decide? Of course
you have. That feeling is a clue. Let it loose, let it flow,
let it carry you forward. This feeling is always right, for it
speaks of something higher than yourself. When this feeling reaches its fullness, it disappears, which is oneness, for

when you stand in the open air, you don't feel the need for air.

Joyce T. said she had felt uncomfortable with herself for a long time, but only recently had she taken action by coming to class. "Wrong decisions are my worst enemy," she confessed. "May I have your comment on this?" Joyce learned, "When your judgment in any matter arises from your purified nature, your original nature, it will be impossible to make decisions against yourself. A rose cannot choose to be a weed."

Never leap this way or that in order to relieve the pressure of indecision. That only gives indecision a temporary hiding place from which it will leap out again and again to annoy you. Instead, remain with not knowing what to do, bear its discomfort consciously. This attracts something entirely new to your mind, something completely above the yes and no of indecision. Then, you will always know what to do.

Sometimes a man looks out at the world's violence and says to himself, "I wish there were another way." Then he mistakenly adds, "But, if there were another way, some men would have found it." He must realize that some men have found it, but he has not met or understood them as yet; he knows only those still under the power of their own violence. In this book you are reading the names and hearing the teachings of men who have found another way.

A VALUABLE LIST FOR DAILY STUDY

The peculiar fact is that people want to change themselves without changing themselves. Examine this strange situation. A man says he wants peace of mind, but refuses to release his resentment toward others which prevents peace. A woman insists she wants to be a better mother to her children, but clings to her moods of depression which is not best. People do not see that to change yourself means to change what you do, who you are, the way you think and react.

See the difference between doctrine and practice. "I must learn about my hidden ways." That is doctrine. "I notice how tense I get when my intelligence is questioned." That is practice. If we live from mere doctrine, we tend to react, "Oh, I already know that I must study my hidden motives. Give me something new." This attitude prevents progress. If you mistakenly believe you have already had lunch, you will not bother to eat—and you will be hungry. This paragraph has deep significance.

Harry W. wanted to know how to speed up his progress. He was told, "Make a definite aim. Aim at more self-knowledge, at freedom from impulsive speech, at anything of value. You have plenty of psychic energy. Everyone does. But just as electricity must have a specific purpose, like lighting a lamp, your energy must be aimed toward a creative result."

A man dwelling in psychic sleep puts demands upon himself which trap and punish him, though he may feel that the pressure originates from outside. This is the tense state of the man who thinks he must make wise statements or witty remarks, or the woman who feels it necessary to make a good impression on others. A teacher of Zen or Taoism would comment, "See what you do against yourself while trying to do something for yourself? Learn the secret of non-action, which is true action."

To remain quiet is true action, the kind of action which delivers understanding. Become aware of noise, both external and internal, and you will see how we depend upon uproars to distract us from what we hesitate to face. We don't trust quietness because it is so foreign to our everyday ways; we prefer the misery of familiarity. Any friendly steps taken toward quietness will be returned with equal friendliness.

A book-lover in Florida had a private library on hundreds of subjects, collected over the years. He suddenly became overwhelmingly interested in anything which was rare—rare animals, rare gems, and so on. So from that time on he collected only those books which informed him of rare items. We must be as selective in the collection of ideas, gathering only those which harmonize with our spiritual aims.

Study this list regularly: The great beginning: *a wish for freedom*. The great virtue: *self-honesty*. Great encouragement: *actual self-transformation*. Great barrier: *refusal to listen*. Great technique: *self-awareness*. Great support: *the truth itself*. Great error: *self-centeredness*. Great inspiration: *sensing rightness*. Great aim: *self-knowledge*. Great despair: *feeling separated*. Great healing: *of painful illusion*. Great aid: *patient investigation*. Great correction: *self-correction*. Great result: *self-liberty*.

THE SECRET OF EFFORTLESS ACTION

How can you do these things? Remember, if you really *see* you will really *do*, for there is no difference in the two. The divided mind always projects its own nature, that is, it divides everything, including the division between the *seer* and the *doer*. But in reality, a person is not divided; he is one with himself. As this becomes clear, you *do*—effortlessly and without self-concern.

A scientist understands what it means to be a scientist— because he *is* one. Likewise, we understand the truth by *being* it. As a man dissolves his fictitious sense of self he becomes the truth and the truth becomes him. This is what is meant by self-unity. English author Owen Meredith describes the person who succeeds at this task: "Content to know and be unknown: Whole in himself."

One student commented, "I want freedom from my false self, but do not know what to do." Response: "You are chained to your false self only when you think about it, when you try to expand or protect it. Anger and anxiety arise whenever the false self feels threatened. Detect this in yourself. Eventually, you will realize that this false self is not your friend, as you supposed, but the very root of all your griefs. This detection is right action."

Remember, the right procedure along the path is to never stop and settle down. The wise traveler observes all the alluring sights along the way, but never seeks a sense of security by building a home next to them. He knows what to do when hearing an invitation to pause along the wayside—he listens even more intently to another voice, which is always straight ahead.

You will find yourself not forgetting quite so often. You will slide out of bed remembering your secret life, which then easily handles the daily tasks. You will remember that you can have all the friends you want, but must live your inner life as if you had none. If timid about letting go of fixed ideas, you remember to let go anyway, just to see what happens. You sense what is ahead—a state where you not only know, but know all the time.

Everything good for us exists already. We need not create anything; we need only be conscious of our everpresent oneness with creation. Time does not exist. You can now be what you might have been. Do not take this merely as lofty philosophy; take it as a fact. We see the fact by constantly checking and revising our visual direction. If we look in the direction of the stars, they will be there.

ADVENTURES WITH AUTHENTIC ACTION

1. Profitable action arises from psychic understanding.
2. Become aware of society's artificial actions.
3. There is no way to take advantage of a self-free man.
4. The self-unified man possesses a powerful efficiency.
5. Call the bluff on anything which tries to frighten you.
6. Nothing but good can come from your cosmic voyage.
7. Self-awakening is the one great adventure in life.
8. Notice how perfectly sensible these ideas become.
9. You are capable of being a totally new kind of person.
10. An awakened mind knows the secret of effortless action.

CHAPTER 14

HOW TO LIVE THE LIFE
YOU ALWAYS WANTED

Perhaps you have also asked the question asked by men and women throughout the centuries: "How can I succeed in finding a totally new life?" The answer is both simple and profound: Proceed sincerely with your self-work in spite of all mental confusions and emotional hurts. Do this and you cannot fail. Read it again, but this time try to feel its simple depth: *Proceed sincerely with your self-work in spite of all mental confusions and emotional hurts.*

A wanderer sought entrance to a prosperous country. In an attempt to make himself worthy, he dressed himself in a bright and colorful uniform and presented himself to the border guard. Denied entrance, he changed to three other uniforms, but was turned down each time. When telling the guard, "But I am out of uniforms," the guard replied, "Now you qualify. Come in." We must come to the truth exactly as we are, for there is no other way to come. The truth cares nothing about external appearances; its only requirement is a sincere heart.

No doubt you can see why sincerity is such a gem. Nothing can stop a truly sincere man. Sincerity is always on hand to advise and correct when a man does something wrong or foolish. It is something he can listen to when all else fails. Sincerity can be simply defined. It is the wish, above all other wishes, to make room for the true, regardless of how many of yesterday's ideas must be tossed out.

Dr. William B. said, "It is interesting to hear we must give up personal positions, such as on social questions. Please explain." Reply: "If you give up your side of a social argument, you lose the self-identity this position provides, for example, you can no longer call yourself a liberal or a conservative. This abandonment of a label is too frightening for most people, for they falsely believe they *consist* of their labels, so they fear for their very existence. But it is precisely the self-labeling which causes fear. When you do not have a position which is opposed by another position, life is truly understood, and that is mental wholeness."

Millions of people ask themselves the frustrating question, "In spite of endless searchings, why have I failed to find the contentment of truth?" Why? Because we cannot hear a diamond, nor can we taste a breeze. An entirely new psychic sense must be awakened. Old and familiar ways of thinking cannot receive the new and the unfamiliar. How is this sense awakened? By wanting it with an intensity that would remain if no one else on earth wanted it.

Mental health loves the individual; it does not associate with crowds. The larger the quantity of people, the lower the quality of psychological soundness, which anyone with insight can observe in the massive audience, the overpopulated city, the crowded office. A poem by Robert Frost entitled *THE ROAD NOT TAKEN* tells about a choice which can be made between two roads. It was the less-traveled road which made a great difference.

HOW TO BE TRULY INSPIRED

Said a teacher who gave classes in a grove of cypress trees, "If your watch shows the wrong time, what do you do about it? Well, you don't ask your neighbors to set their watches according to yours; you correct your watch. Unfortunately, you do not make a similar correction when your lives go wrong. Instead, you insist that reality should conform to your illusions. Before you leave this grove, I wish each of you to think deeply about this error.''

A man lives truly only when he knows what it means to live from himself. When a person in a crowd appears cheery and confident, it is unlikely that he possesses those virtues in fact. In almost every case he is merely imitating the contrived gaiety of others; he is unconsciously absorbing the artificial atmosphere. Set him among gloomy people and his mechanical mind clicks out the command, ''Time to be sad,'' which he slavishly obeys. Such a man is made by his surroundings, never by himself.

You don't need to be dragged around by an unwanted self; not when you really understand. You need to understand that this self by which you identify yourself is not you at all. You are not your acquired opinions and habits and material possessions. You are not separate from anyone else on earth. You are one with the One.

Harry T., an athletic coach, commented, ''You say that reality frees us from feeling offended. How does it work?'' Reply: ''What gets offended? Imaginary virtues. The very feeling of being offended proves that the particular virtue exists only in fantasy. You can praise an actor's stage performance, but it is risky to ask him how he acts at home. It is impossible to offend an imageless man. Would you like to be such a man?''

The false sense of self stands as a distorting screen between us and reality. Incoming impressions are distorted according to personal desires and motives, thus preventing a freely flowing exchange between us and external events. With the removal of the false self, we no longer see ourselves as separate from whatever comes to us, which is complete mental, psychological, and spiritual health.

In this book I have offered several examples of a curious fact: Man fears that inflowing truth will harm him, and so he resists it fiercely. His chief fear is that truth will rob him of his false sense of self, which is the very root of all his sorrows. A miserable man fears that truth will steal away his happiness! In your self-work, remember that truthful impressions finally result in the exact opposite of what negative whisperings try to tell you. Instead of losing yourself, you find yourself.

A significant event takes place in the psychic system every time we hear the truth. The hearing immediately turns into a feeling. When hearing the truth and wanting the truth we receive a positive impression. This is authentic inspiration. When hearing a truth while not wanting it a psychic collision occurs, injuring us. These eventful hearings of the truth occur a hundred times a day, but are noticed and used wisely only by the self-working person. The way you take what happens should occupy all your attention and interest.

TECHNIQUE FOR SELF-PROGRESS

We crowd ourselves into every corner of life for fear we will miss something. In this we are like an artist who spoils his painting by cramming too many figures into it. We rarely pause to ask what it would be like to relax from the scramble, for above all we fear relaxation. As long as a man falsely assumes the existence of a self *and* life, he will also assume a false and frantic responsibility for keeping his life moving. The cure is to see that life moves itself, which oneness with life discloses.

Your first responsibility in life is to live a life of truth. Do that and you will never have any of the false responsibilities which burden and confuse most people. You are never required to shoulder the responsibility of those who refuse to take responsibility for themselves. If you are presently weighted by doing what you do not want to do, there is good news for you. By making the truth your first responsibility, you will see the last of needless responsibility.

A tennis player stays within the court's boundary lines in order to avoid a penalty. But suppose he obeyed the lines after the game, being fearful of stepping off the court?

You would rightly think him hypnotized. Millions are hypnotized by mankind's mechanical rules, not having the slightest knowledge that the tense game can be called off any time they like. Think about this. Think about calling off the mechanical game, after which you can walk wherever you like.

There is a right way and a wrong way to detach yourself from wrong people and circumstances. If you use your habitual mind to escape from them you will eventually find yourself right back in similar involvements, for the habitual mind always attracts its own nature. The right way is to first attain a mental state of detachment, which appears as you *deeply* see the self-harm of your present circumstances. Then, the necessary physical departure will be clear and easy. This high state of understanding keeps you forever free of harmful involvements.

Loretta J. said she had read dozens of philosophers, naming Shankara, Pythagoras, Goethe, and Descartes. She wondered how to turn her knowledge into maximum value. "There is great value," she was told, "in letting the facts change the self—a deep and personal change which leaves no room for self-confusion. A philosophy has value only if it changes the philosopher."

Take time for this profitable experiment. Hold your place on this page and turn back to any other page in the book. Select and read any paragraph on this earlier page. Now, see the connection between the main thought of this paragraph and the thought of any selected paragraph on this page. There will be a definite connection, for the truth is undivided, it is whole. It is like putting several letters of the alphabet together to form a complete word. Practice this surprisingly effective technique frequently.

HOW TO ENTER A NEW WORLD

I wonder whether you are sufficiently impressed with the need to cut loose the false sense of self? Let's review. A man worriedly asks, "How can I save myself?" and

"What shall I do with myself?" But what if he is not the self he thinks he is? In that case a thousand worried questions collapse like old buildings whose foundations have been blasted away. He is not the self he thinks he is, and when seeing this, worries no longer have a home in his mind.

Realize your ability to calmly observe a crisis instead of reacting to it in the usual ways. Are you aware of how you can pause to observe an event before going on to the word or act or feelings? Try to do it and see how possible it is. The pausing, the waiting, the observing—that is what transforms your world by first transforming you. If the habitual and mechanical response does not arise, another response will take its place. This fresh response will be in your favor, for it disconnects you from yesterday.

You win by losing. People find this esoteric fact very strange at first, but it can turn into a marvelous revelation. In the everyday world we win by gaining a new home or friend or excitement, but we must reverse this process when dealing with the inner world. Think of something you would like to lose. See how its loss would be a win for you? This is the idea. Our objective is to lose mental mists, which give us a clear inner world, which then duplicates itself outwardly.

If you have the possibility for an interior storm, it will be aroused by an exterior storm, for both vibrate on the same psychic level. But if through self-insight you have achieved mental fair-weather, there is no way for an extior storm to touch you, for you reside above its lower vibrations. Do not take this merely as an illustration, nor as philosophic idealism, but as a practical fact which can become your healing experience.

"Please tell me whether I understand a certain point," said one inquirer. "Self-change begins with self-observation. In order to change what we are, we must first see what we are. Is that right?" Reply: "Right. By standing too close to a mirror you are unable to see yourself clearly. To get a good look you must stand back a bit. Self-change begins the moment you can distinguish between your actual state and your imaginary state. Because this is somewhat upsetting at first, many people will not do it. You do it, and you won't be chained like many people.''

Study these facts about the suppression of negative ideas: 1. The deeper the suppression of a negative and false idea, the greater the self-damage. 2. The depth of the suppression of a wrong idea will be equaled by the hostile denial of its existence. 3. Suppression appears to provide self-security, but since the protected self is imaginary, suppression produces insecurity. 4. Awareness of suppression begins to lift it. 5. There can be no harm at all in becoming aware of suppression; it only appears that way at first. 6. The absence of all suppression is total mental health.

LEARN TO SERVE YOUR TRUE INTERESTS

''In past classes,'' said a real estate agent, ''you provided us with different ways to begin self-transformation. I find them very interesting. May we have another?'' Reply: ''Ask yourself whether it is possible that your entire life up to now has been a gigantic hoax which you have unconsciously played on yourself. Have the courage to do this and self-change begins at once.''

We have already seen how fiercely a man fights any attempt of true teachers to destroy his haunted house. But why this strange and illogical behavior? Because he fears its destruction will turn him out into a terrifying world. He never notices how terrified he is already! But as his eyes begin to open, he is filled with a great yearning to escape, and this yearning is both a step and a strength. Then, abandoning his false feeling of security, he learns to say with Emerson, ''There is always safety in valor.''

A man always feels as if he is standing on a trap door, but rarely has the insight to step off it because he calls it an attractice carpet. A man must see for himself that exterior gains do nothing for his inner contentment. He must realize that the attainment of his goals or his demands produces only a short-lived thrill which he mistakes for happiness. Such insight is an explosive power toward his awakening to authentic happiness.

It is very strange, but the last thing which interests people is their own true interests. This is because people do not know their true nature. Not realizing their natural blending with all of life, they cannot have an interest in the facts which could reveal this happy condition to them. So not seeing what is right, they pour their interest into what is wrong, ending up in suppressed tears and tension every time. This is why the mystic masters teach, "Nothing awakens a man from psychic sleep faster than to glimpse how that sleep punishes him."

A harbor with a narrow opening can admit only small ships with a limited value of cargo. A wider opening permits larger cargoes of greater wealth. There we have an excellent illustration of why openness to valuable realities should be complete openness. Open yourself to this rich thought: If a depressed person were to ask himself the reason for his depression—and was ruthlessly scientific about it—he would be unable to find a reason. He could come up with a reply, but never a reason, for in reality there is none.

Once we know, we must do. We know we must observe each thought and feeling as it arises, then let it fade out in its natural manner. We must not cling to thoughts and feelings just because they stimulate us. That causes clogging, which prevents a spontaneous flow of the psychic system. Now that you know—do! It will save years of weary search.

PATHWAYS TO TOTAL HEALING

If we wish a truth to turn into a healing force, we must receive it with all of our psychological parts. Simply hearing a truth does not change us, any more than hearing a symphony turns us into a musician. A man wrongly assumes he understands a truth merely because he has absorbed it into his memory, so when hearing a truth that could heal him he dismisses it with, "But I already heard that." To receive truth with whole-heartedness means a willingness to give up something wrong in us in exchange for what is right for us.

We must see the difference between self-will and cosmic-will. Self-will is powerless and ruinous. It wants what it wants, regardless of the consequences to others or to itself. It is composed of ignorance, cunning, egotism. Cosmic-will starts with a wish to escape the dreadful tyranny of self-will. Cosmic-will feels the wrong in what used to be called right, it begins to listen to new voices, it senses another world.

Said Alan B., "I am interested in what you say about saving energy for the inner task. Please comment." Reply: "Suppose you hear the rumor that there are vicious bears in the nearby woods, so you nervously and endlessly build protections around your home. When learning there are no bears at all, you save much time and energy for useful tasks. Likewise, when realizing that ego-protection is utterly pointless, you save precious energy for inner exploration."

Be on constant guard against wrong conclusions. For example, this book uses thousands of familiar words, but familiarity with words does not necessarily indicate familiarity with the deeper meanings behind the words. We may understand what is meant by the word "astronomy" and yet know nothing about the stars and planets themselves. We can avoid wrong conclusions by seeing that the use of words like "strength" and "liberty" are not the same as actually possessing inner strength and liberty.

Start today to give the word "success" a totally different meaning. Disconnect it entirely from its usual definitions, such as financial profit. See a successful day as one in which you observed yourself frequently, while reacting with neither pain nor pleasure at what you observed. Perhaps you observe a sudden pang of loneliness, which prompts you to call a friend. Maybe you unreel a mental movie of how you hope a future event will turn out. Just watch such inner movements as they happen. New feelings enter as you do this, feelings which make "success" mean something brightly different.

An American scientist was sent to a remote island in the Pacific Ocean to study the air currents in the region. Finding the air to be extraordinarily pure and refreshing, he filled a bottle with some of it. Upon returning home he placed the sealed bottle in a prominent place in his home. When asked about it he said it was his reminder of the existence of pure air. Let these paragraphs remind you of the existence of psychic purity and refreshment.

HOW TO USE THIS BOOK PROFITABLY

Wagon trains of the early West employed scouts to send back messages about the unknown territory ahead. One scout mistakenly reported the absence of hostile Indians, but corrected himself in time to prevent disaster. Every moment you tell yourself about yourself. Have you ever noticed this? We must make sure our messages are accurate. You could not send yourself a more helpfully accurate message than this: "I may not really understand something which I now believe I understand. I will search it out."

To do what he wants to do is every man's idea of a supremely happy life. It is possible. A man can have that supremacy. All he needs to do is abolish false wants. This comes by abolishing false ideas about oneself, for example, that it is good to have power over another. Whoever has dismissed false wants cannot harm himself or others. In this state of self-unity, he has no other way to live except as he wants, for nature's wants and his are the same.

For the sake of study, we use opposite terms such as inner and outer, conscious and unconscious, spiritual and material. But we must remember that life is actually unified, whole, with no divided parts. It is a divided mind which divides life, and then claims one part for itself exclusively. It is like two small brothers with one apple. Each sees only his half of the apple, but their mother sees the whole apple. A whole mind sees the whole because it *is* the whole.

A persistent discontent with ourselves as we are is the first call to the other way of life. When feeling this discontent sharply, we can then make one of the great decisions of our life. It is the decision to change ourselves, instead of trying to change the exterior world, which changes nothing. It is challenging work at times, but is also a lot of fun. Above all, it is really the only sensible task we have here on earth.

Let your mind ring with the declaration, "Healing always takes place when I cease to interfere with the natural healing process." How do we unwisely interfere? Mainly by insisting upon using artificial remedies manufactured by the conditioned mind. Careful observation exposes them. Sidney C. observed his willingness to accept counsel as long as it agreed with what he already believed. When he saw how yesterday's habits interfered with today's healing, healing began.

As you study the principles in this book over the weeks and years, do the following: 1. Study with a receptive mind which wants above all else to know the truth which sets us free. 2. Read with a light yet serious mind, just as you might lightly yet earnestly learn to swim. 3. Receive these ideas without the interference of previously formed beliefs and conclusions. 4. Let each new reading reveal fresh information and inspiration, which will surely come to the mind which welcomes them.

THE MARVEL OF AN AWAKENED MIND

Cecil H. came with a question which showed good insight. He asked, "How can we lose interest in fascinating things which are bad for us?" He gained more insight by hearing, "If you gain a tree bearing an abundant harvest of oranges, you quicly lose all interest in an attractive but fruitless tree. Gain just one spiritual orange for yourself, taste it, and see how that fruitful tree takes all your interest and your time. Wrongness has no chance whatever against rightness."

To discover what must be changed in ourselves is not a dreary task; it is a delightful excursion. What is more pleasant than to change from slavery to a habit to command of that habit? What is more delightful than to switch from tension in a human relationship to calm communication? If we could just see that work *on* ourselves is work *for* ourselves!

Good news is ours whenever we remember a certain prominent theme in higher teachings. The theme proclaims the existence of internal restfulness, regardless of external chaos and defeat. To see this restfulness is to experience it. Sri Ramana Maharshi, who taught at Arunachala, India, likened peace to a pond which cannot be seen because it is covered with weeds. Remove the weeds and the cooling water is ours. Remove the veils from our minds and bliss is ours.

The marvel of an awakened mind! A true teacher occupies a lofty level which would amaze all the professors and scholars in the world—if they could only understand him. A scholar may have great intellectual knowledge of a particular subject, perhaps psychology or religion, science or semantics. However, he remains confined to his single room of knowledge, while the awakened man roams the entire cosmic college. He has shattered the walls of words which restrict others, to see reality in its healthy totality.

We must impress ourselves with the need for right attitudes toward the lofty principles which come our way. One right attitude is to see them as *instructive invitations*. In telling a parable, Jesus presented this perfect instructive invitation: "Friend, go up higher." Remember, we can always understand anything we are willing to understand.

A hiker was lost in the mountains. For three days he

huddled at the base of a hill to protect himself from uncomfortable winds. Deciding to defy the winds in order to look around, he climbed the hill. At once he saw a signal light which had been set up by a rescue team three days before. Likewise, our rescue light is always available. By daring to change our inner position, we sight it instantly.

Do you remember the first paragraph of Chapter 1? Read it again.

TEN GUIDES TO DAILY INSPIRATION

1. Continue with your inner adventure in spite of everything.
2. The only requirement for self-healing is a sincere mind.
3. You can develop a new sense for hearing cosmic truth.
4. Psychic health comes to the individual, not to the crowd.
5. You are not required to surrender yourself to society.
6. Calmly observe a crisis, instead of falling into it.
7. A self-unified human being is a successful human being.
8. Remember the purity and refreshment of these principles.
9. Let natural healing forces enter to do their good work.
10. Remain alert, and you will sight your new world at last.

About Vernon Howard

Vernon Howard is a unique teacher who broke through to another world. He sees through the illusion of suffering and fear and loneliness. For many years his popular books and lectures on the inner-life have all centered around the one grand topic: "There is a way out of the human problem and any earnest person can find it."

His books are widely used by doctors, psychologists, clergymen, educators and people from all walks of life. More than seven million grateful readers have experienced the power of Mr. Howard's books, including translations into a number of languages. Vernon Howard's clear insight into human nature and his practical solutions attract thousands of new readers worldwide every year.

Informal study groups of men and women use Mr. Howard's books and listen to his taped lectures. For more information, write today to:

New Life, PO Box 2230, Pine, Arizona 85544

Please send us
the names and addresses of friends
who may be interested in these teachings.

Praise for Vernon Howard